Management accounting for Marketing and Business

a profit oriented approach

RICHARD KOTAS,
BCom, MPhil, ACIS, FBHA
Schiller International University

HUTCHINSON

Hutchinson Education

An imprint of Century Hutchinson Ltd
62–65 Chandos Place
London WC2N 4NW

Century Hutchinson, Australia Pty Ltd
89–91 Albion Street, Surry Hills,
New South Wales 2010, Australia

Century Hutchinson New Zealand Limited
PO Box 40-086, Glenfield, Auckland 10,
New Zealand

Century Hutchinson South Africa (Pty) Ltd
PO Box 337, Bergvlei, 2012 South Africa

First published 1989

Set in Plantin and Univers

by Activity Ltd, Salisbury, Wilts

Printed and bound in Great Britain by
Butler & Tanner.Ltd, Frome and London

British Library Cataloguing in Publication Data
Kotas, Richard
  Accounting for marketing business.
  1. Management accounting
  I. Title
  658.1'511

ISBN 0–09–172968–8

To Stefan, Anna, Zosia and Filip

Dear Student...

With courses becoming more and more intensive there is a greater need for students to have. *precise study information* available so that they can study more efficiently and speedily.

At the same time this enables *tutors* to devote more effort towards the understanding and analysis of the subject. Rather than give up valuable time dictating and providing notes, they can concentrate more on actively involving students in the learning process.

In this text the author has covered all aspects of coursework providing:

- A comprehensive text on the subject
- Self assessment tests
- Past examination questions
- Worked examples throughout the text
- Answers to self assessment tests

The combination of these elements will greatly improve your confidence and performance in the examinations.

Contents

Preface

The aim of the present volume is to provide a basic text in management accounting for students following courses in business studies and marketing. The text differs from the majority of existing books on the subject in two respects. First, there is a tendency for all management accounting books to draw on examples from the manufacturing industries. With the decline of many traditional manufacturing industries, it is now appropriate to shift the emphasis to the service industries, which have grown in stature and importance in recent years. In addition, therefore, to some of the more traditional examples students will find throughout the present volume, numerous references to and examples from theatres, leisure centres, hotels, travel agents as well as retailing operations.

Secondly, most management accounting texts – however competently written – tend to neglect two important areas of study: pricing and profitability. It is hoped that both lecturers and students will welcome Chapter 12 on Profit Sensitivity Analysis, which is based on the author's recent research, and Chapter 13 on Pricing, which should appeal to all students – and students of marketing in particular. Chapter 14, entitled Responsibility Accounting, complements the chapter on budgeting and introduces the student to an important aspect of management accounting which is not referred to in most of the existing texts.

I am grateful to the Association of Business Executives, the Institute of Commercial Management, the Institute of Marketing and Schiller International University for permission to include some of their past examination questions. Also I wish to thank Miss Jacqueline Chung, BSc, a post-graduate student at Schiller International University for proof reading the book. Last, but by no means least, I am indebted to my daughter-in-law, Janine, for her unfailing patience in typing the manuscript.

London, 1988   Richard Kotas

General study and exam tips

"In many situations information is so great a part of effectiveness that without information a really clever person cannot get started. With information a much less clever person can get very far." Dr Edward De Bono.

Being successful on a course does not simply result from listening to lectures or reading a textbook. You must become actively involved in the learning process in order to acquire knowledge and skills and perform well in assessments.

There is no reason why you cannot achieve this aim. After all you are on a course of study because an examining authority believes that you have the necessary ability to complete the course successfully. If you are prepared to become actively involved and do the work required, you have every right to feel confident that you can succeed in the final examinations.

These notes are designed to make your study more efficient, to ensure that you use this manual to best advantage and to help you improve both your coursework and your examination techniques. They have been divided into four parts:

1 general study tips
2 improving the quality of your work
3 examination technique
4 studying with this text

■ 1   GENERAL STUDY TIPS

An eminent physicist once said: 'Thinking is 99 per cent perspiration and 1 per cent inspiration'. Take his advice and that of most of us who have had the benefit of a good education. Ignore the advice of those who believe you can prepare yourself for the examination in one or two weeks. Knowledge and skills of any value are not easily learned. For most of us it takes time to understand and permanently remember the content of a subject; instead of forgetting everything immediately the examinations are over. Therefore start working at studying right at the very start of your course and continue at a steady pace until the examinations. Do all the work expected of you by your tutor including homework and mock/mid term examinations. Homework is good practice and the mock exams simulate aspects of the final examination. Doing them as best as you can makes your tutor more willing to help you, as he or she will see that you are playing your part in the learning process.

The knowledge and skills you will gain on your course of study are precisely the kind needed by professional business people. So approach the study of each subject as if you were in real life a business man or woman, or a person following a profession such as accountancy or law. In this way the subject should come alive for you, and your motivation to learn should increase.

To help realise this objective, read a quality daily and Sunday newspaper that has a good business section. By doing this you will discover what is happening on a day-to-day basis and be in a better position to understand the topics you are studying on the course. You will also broaden and deepen your knowledge of the subject. Professional people at work usually read a quality newspaper and monthly or quarterly periodical related directly to their discipline in order to keep abreast of the latest developments. You will probably wish to do the same when you commence work, so why not start now?

Carry a pocket dictionary with you and look up words you hear or read but do not understand. None of us has a complete vocabulary but we can improve it if we really want to be able to read and study more effectively. In the case of students it is even more important because words used in lectures, textbooks or newspapers often become misused in examinations. Some words which cause problems with their meaning or spelling are:

aggregate	disseminate	heterogeneous
antithesis	distinguish	homogenous
constituent	evaluate	panacea
discipline	facsimile	prognosis

Do you fully understand how these words may be used in the context of your subject? Use a dictionary.

As soon as you start your course, find out if you are going to be given past examination reports for your subject, examiners' reports, specimen answers to previous examination questions and a work scheme. It is probable that they will not all be available at your school, college or university or even from the examining authority. You should, however, obtain as much information about your course of study and the examinations as possible so you know exactly what amount of work lies ahead of you and the academic standard you are expected to reach. This will help in planning your personal workload for the period of your course.

If you do not understand something ask your tutor. Do not assume that you are inadequate because you did not understand something that other students seemed to appreciate. They may be having difficulties too or your lecturer may simply not have explained the point to everyone's satisfaction. If something is overlooked by the tutor, don't be afraid to bring it to his/her attention.

Personal health is something that many students dismiss with comments such as: 'what has health got to do with ability to think?' Studies on the topic have now clearly indicated that general health and mental performance are statistically related. Within four weeks of being given multi vitamin and mineral tablets students in two separate controlled studies improved upon their written performance in intelligence tests by approximately ten points. Your common-sense alone should tell you that you cannot perform at your best if you continually feel tired or have flu or a heavy cold in an examination. Eat a varied diet that includes protein foods, vegetables and fruit, and get some daily exercise even if it is only a good brisk walk home after your day's study.

Contrary to the belief of many students, the best academic work is not done at night-time. Once again research shows that students perform better in the early part of the week, in the daytime – particularly mornings – and in a place where there is natural daylight to read and write by. Therefore plan your study schedule so that it is completed in the day. This will also leave you the evenings and weekends free to relax and enjoy yourself.

■ 2 IMPROVING THE QUALITY OF YOUR WORK

The earlier in the course you bring your work to a satisfactory standard the more likely you are to exhibit a good standard of work in the examinations. Obviously, academic standards do relate to the thinking abilities of the student but they also depend on motivation, and a logical approach to one's work if effective presentation at the appropriate academic standard is to be achieved. Here are three tips that will help you develop a logical approach to the presentation of your work.

Read the question carefully

When undertaking essay or numerical work make sure you read the question very carefully. Underline the key words in the question so that your mind is concentrated on the essential aspects. For example, distinguish between the two main types of question.

DESCRIPTIVE QUESTIONS
A descriptive question is one in which you will be expected to describe or explain something and possibly distinguish it from alternative or similar items or ideas. Two examples are:
(a) *Describe* the *benefits* of *budgetary control* and explain the additional *advantages* of *zero-based* budgeting.

(b) *Explain,* with the *aid of a break-even chart, how the price* of a product *influences* the *break-even point.*

Some of the key words have been emphasised in italics to give you an idea of which words are at the heart of the question. Always underline or highlight the key words yourself before attempting to answer.

ANALYTICAL QUESTIONS

These include the purely analytical questions, or the analytical question that requires you to evaluate a statement (indicate your level of support for an idea/give it a value) or present your own ideas. Examples of these are:

(a) *Solely analytical:* Analyse the contention that there is no such thing as fixed costs.

(b) *Analytical and Evaluative:* How far do you support the idea that adult behaviour is predominantly related to one's early childhood experiences?

If you have been presented with a minicase (short story) or a case study (extended story) detailing opposing opinions regarding a problem a company is faced with, you may be requested to offer your own solution. In this event your answer should analyse the value of all the opinions offered in the case as well as possibly suggesting your own.

Consider also the way a question is structured. If it is in two or more parts give equal time to each if equal marks are awarded to each part. If more marks are awarded to one part than another, allocate your time in the same proportions as the marks awarded. For example, if a Question has marks awarded: part (a) 5 marks, part (b) 15 marks (total 20 marks), you should spend a quarter (5/20) of your time answering (a) and three quarters (15/20) on (b).

Sometimes the time you should allocate to a part of a question is indicated by the implied requirements of the question, rather than by marks. For example

Q1 (a) Briefly outline what you understand by a profit centre.
   (b) Give two examples of natural profit centres and two examples of artificial profit centres and explain the effect of the latter on motivation.

By using the words 'briefly outline' the examiner is indicating that much less time should be spent on answering part (a). The question requires more marks to be awarded to part (b) as the analytical and applied nature of this part indicates that it is more difficult to answer.

With numerical type questions, such as in accountancy and statistics, do not assume that all you have to do is arrive at the right answer. Your tutor – or an examiner – will expect you to explain what you are doing as you introduce each set of workings, graphs, illustrations or tables. After all, how is your tutor to know how you arrived at the right answer if you do not explain? Even more importantly, even if you give the wrong answer, at least you will be given some marks for those parts of your calculation which are correct. Such subjects involve a large element of communication and if you do not communicate effectively in your answer what you are doing you will lose marks.

Construct an essay plan

Always spend a few minutes constructing an essay plan before answering a question. This only requires jotting down a few notes for each paragraph which indicates the approach you will take to your answer and the points you will include. This will make sure that you construct your essay in a logical manner and that you keep to a target when writing your answer.

Follow up with your tutor

To understand fully what is required when answering questions, ask your tutor about the work you have handed in and had marked if he or she has not commented sufficiently on your script, informing you of where you were right and wrong and why.

3   EXAMINATION TECHNIQUE

If you are studying at college you can start improving your examination technique in the mock/mid term examination which will help you in the coursework assessment during the second half of the course as well as in the final examination. Here are a few tips on improving your presentation.

- *Always do rough workings*. Use essay plans and/or numerical workings to plan your answer, but on a page other than the one on which you start your answer to the question. Cross through your rough working before starting to answer the question.
- Select the questions you intend to answer and *start with the one you think you will find the easiest to answer*. In this way you may gain your highest marks early in the exam which is very important in case you do not complete the examination.
- *Keep an eye on the clock* so that you allow about the same amount of time for answering each question (unless one is a more difficult, compulsory question). Noting the time in order to complete all the questions you are required to answer gives you a better chance of achieving high marks.
- Allow at least a third to half a page for illustrations or diagrams. In this way they look like illustrations rather than scribblings and you have sufficient space available if you have to return to your illustration to add more detail later in the examination. Always explain what your illustration is supposed to illustrate.
- Unless otherwise instructed, use a complete page of graph paper for presenting graphs and make sure that you provide a title for any entries you have made. Explain what your graph illustrates.
- Do not present workings for numerical subjects such as accounts and statistics without explaining what you are doing and why.

If you would like a deeper understanding of study skills and exam techniques a useful book containing a wealth of tips and examples that will help you to succeed in examinations is *How To Pass Exams* by W G Leader, also published by Hutchinson.

■ 4   STUDYING WITH THIS TEXT

Hutchinson's student texts have been specifically designed to act as study aids for students while on a course, as well as present the contents of a subject in a way that is both interesting and informative.

Use this text as part of your study activities, adding your own or your tutor's notes at appropriate points. Study your textbook in great detail, making notes on the chief points in each chapter so that the ideas have gone through your own head and down onto the paper in your own words – though perhaps with key quotations from the text.

Don't get bogged down in any one chapter. If you really can't follow the chapter leave it and go on to the next, returning at a later date. What seems difficult at the start of your course in September will be easier by December and child's play by March! You are going to develop as you do the course – so don't give up too early. Perseverance is everything in acquiring professional status.

Do not just read the specimen answers provided at the end of certain sections. Study their content and structure in the light of what you learned in the particular section and what you learned earlier in this section. In this way your skill in answering questions set by your tutor and/or the examination should improve.

At the end of each section there are examples of past examination questions. Where the answer is to be in essay form jot down beside the question the major points that you think should have been highlighted when answering. Then check back with the appropriate text of the particular section to see if your answer would have been correct. If you are still uncertain, discuss the problem with your tutor.

Talking with the tutor and fellow students is essential for developing the ability to analyse problems.

Always complete the Self Assessment part of each chapter as they are designed to reinforce what you have learned and improve your recall of the topics. Check your answers with those provided in the manual. As repetition of a process improves one's memory, it is very useful to re-test yourself every few weeks or let someone else read the questions to you and tell you if you got them right.

If the subject covered by the particular manual involves value judgements do not assume that what is mentioned in the manual is the only correct version. Your tutor may have other opinions which are just as valid. What matters is that you have sufficient knowledge of the subject to illustrate a firm understanding of the topic in the examinations.

One of the best ways to study is to buy a lever arch file and make out dividing pages from brown paper for each subject or chapter. File your notes, and your essays and any newspaper cuttings, articles, etc. that are relevant in the appropriate topic position. You will then have an easy to revise and lively set of notes. If you find it a bit bulky to carry, use a ring binder instead and then at the end of every week or two weeks transfer the notes you have made to the lever arch file, keeping it at home for safety.

Now that you have read these Study and Exam Tips you should feel confident to continue with your studies and succeed in the examinations. It just remains for Hutchinson and myself to wish you every success on your course.

☐1☐ **Introduction**

■ BRANCHES AND ORIENTATIONS OF ACCOUNTING

Historical accounting

For a long time and until quite recently accounting was characterized by a backward-looking approach; and the accountant was regarded as a chronicler of past events. At the beginning of each accounting year a business would open a new set of books. Transactions would then be recorded until the end of the year, when the accountant (or the external auditors) would draw up the profit and loss account and the balance sheet.

The main characteristic of this practice was its preoccupation with past events; effective techniques for dealing with the present and the future were yet to be developed. This, now out-of-date, approach – sometimes described as 'historical accounting' – is no longer practised except in some very small businesses.

Cost accounting

Throughout the nineteenth century and until recently the UK was the workshop of the world, with numerous and extensive manufacturing activities necessitating the evolution of costing methods, without which a rational conduct of an industrial enterprise would have been impossible.

Cost accounting, as we know it today, has three main functions:

1 To record current costs;
2 To analyse such costs in relation to various products, departments, cost centres, etc;
3 To present cost information to management.

Management accounting, as will be seen later, is in many respects similar to and indeed an extension of cost accounting.

Financial accounting

Whilst cost and management accounting are concerned with the provision of information to persons within the business, financial accounting has the function of supplying information to outside parties, e.g. shareholders, financial institutions, government departments, banks, etc. The second characteristic of financial accounting is that it deals with the business as a whole: creditors, financial institutions, Inland Revenue, etc. are not interested in departmental unit costs, profit margins or departmental performance. What interests them is, essentially, total overall profitability and the availability of cash and liquid resources.

Let us now consider the element of time. Many reports prepared by the financial accountant are concerned with what has already taken place. The preparation of the final accounts and the subsequent calculation of return on capital and other accounting ratios are all activities dealing with the past. A great deal of the work of the management accountant, on the other hand, relates to the present and the future. Thus budgeting, cost and profit estimates, pricing of products and services are all relevant to what is, or is likely to happen in the future. It might, therefore, be tempting to say that whilst financial accounting is backward-looking, management accounting represents a sum total of forward-looking activities. This distinction in time orientation is not however always true. Financial accountants frequently analyse past results in order to make decisions relevant to the future course of business. Similarly management accountants regularly report on past performance of various sections of an enterprise. Whilst, therefore, there is some merit and truth in this distinction, it is certainly not universally valid.

Management accounting

Management accounting has been defined by the Institute of Cost and Management Accountants as 'the presentation of accounting information in such a way as to assist management in the creation of policy and the day-to-day operation of an undertaking'. The main features of management accounting may be summarized as follows:

1   What basically distinguishes management accounting from other branches of accounting is its philosophy and orientation. This finds its expression in the emphasis on the provision of information – and not just cost information – with a view to assisting management in the effective running of the organization.

2   Management accounting – as cost accounting – deals with individual departments, cost and revenue centres and products, rather than the business as a whole. The management accountant will, therefore, spend a great deal of time on activities such as: departmental/product cost analysis; pricing of individual products/activities; reporting on the performance of the various departments, branches or divisions of the business; preparation of functional as well as other budgets, etc.

3 Although the past has general relevance to the present and some relevance to the future, helping departmental managers and top management enjoins an emphasis on the present and the future. Almost all management accounting work is, therefore, characterized by a forward-looking approach, designed to ensure that current management decisions make sense in terms of what will take place next week, next month, etc.

■ FUNCTIONS OF MANAGEMENT

From what has already been said the student will appreciate that, essentially, management accounting is the kind of accounting which is intended to help management manage the business. It is pertinent, therefore, at this stage to look at the functions of management to see how the management accountant can help the management team in: (a) planning; (b) decision making; (c) controlling and (d) evaluating performance.

Planning

Almost all the planning undertaken within the context of a business operation involves scarce resources and entails expenditure. Plans, therefore, cannot be made except on the basis of detailed and relevant information relating to sales volumes, operating costs, profit margins, etc. The routine and probably most important plans which are drawn up from one year to another are *budgets*. It is in the process of budgeting that the involvement of management accountants represents their most important contribution to planning. Before the budgets are prepared it is necessary to make some important decisions on matters such as the budgeted sales volumes, level of prices to be charged during the forthcoming budget period and the required return on capital. Here, too, management accountants have an important role to play in providing appropriate information and thus helping the management team to make these critical decisions without which the budgeting process cannot even be commenced.

Decision making

Some decisions made by managers are regular routine decisions which are made from one day/week to another. A simple example of a routine decision may be given as follows. In order to plan the deployment of the sales force, the marketing manager of a trading organization needs information on sales volumes, sales mix, number of units sold, salespeople employed in each area, etc. Such information would regularly be provided by the management accountant, who alone is responsible for ensuring that the information is accurate, relevant and timely.

Other decisions are of a non-routine nature and these tend to be the more important and difficult decisions. For example:

1 Should the company establish a new operation in an overseas country?
2 Should one of the divisions of the company cease operations during a slack period, and if so for how long a period?
3 Is it desirable to lower the price of a particular product in order to enhance its popularity?

Such non-routine decisions require not only a lot of clear thinking (which should characterize all decision making) but also a lot of relevant information from the management accountant. Quite frequently it will be necessary for the management accountant to undertake a special study/analysis of a problem and write a report to management: (a) explaining the nature of the problem; (b) setting out the various alternative courses of action the company may take and (c) stating clearly the effect of each course of action on profitability, cash position, etc.

Controlling

In this particular function of management all managers rely heavily on the control reports produced by the management accountant. In larger organizations it is usual for the management accountant to produce weekly, monthly, quarterly and other reports on various aspects of the business. Reports which deal with current income and expenditure will, typically, show the budgeted and actual results as well as any variances (deviations of actual from budgeted results). It is such reports that tell the managers whether all operations are proceeding according to plan (company budget). Also it is largely on the basis of such reports that managers decide what, if any, corrective action is required.

Evaluating

In order to evaluate the performance of managers it is essential to develop appropriate standards of performance. Such standards are sometimes difficult to establish as a lot of management activity does not lend itself to easy quantification. Let us look at one or two examples.

Sales managers are frequently evaluated (and remunerated) on the basis of sales volumes achieved. Now and again, however, they may be tempted to secure large orders at uneconomically low prices. Whilst achieving, even exceeding, their sales targets, they may be making little contribution to company profits. Standards of performance for executives such as personnel and training managers, buyers, and indeed accountants, are particularly difficult to set.

There is, nevertheless, a large area of management activity which lends itself to objective evaluation. In all manufacturing organizations the management accountant will rely on company standard costs for materials, labour, etc. and report on current production costs for all cost centres, sales volumes and profit margins achieved as well as contribution of each division/branch to overall company profitability. In trading organizations the management accountant will report on profits achieved by individual product lines. Whilst, therefore, problems of performance evaluation exist, there is certainly a great deal of scope for the management accountant to make an important contribution to this function of management.

■ RELEVANCE OF OPERATIONS

As stated earlier in this chapter, the most important aim of management accounting is to assist management in the efficient and profitable management of operations. If management accountants are to be effective in achieving this aim they must ensure that they take an interest in and are knowledgeable about company business operations. It is essential, therefore, that they do not stand aloof but show an active, on-going interest in all productive and/or trading activities. If they do not acquire a sufficient insight into the nature of the operation they will not be sufficiently familiar with the actual methods of production or trading activities to appreciate the day-to-day problems involved. Without this insight they will not be able to develop a sensible framework of control procedures or design a relevant and logical system of reporting to management.

In helping management to achieve adequate profitability management accountants must, through their insight into operations, acquire a good appreciation of how the business makes its profits. As explained in Chapter 12 on Profit Sensitivity Analysis, in some businesses profits are very sensitive to operating costs; in other businesses it is the revenue side of the business that has a dominant effect on profitability. In cost-sensitive operations, therefore, management accountants will spend a considerable amount of time on cost analysis, cost control and the presentation of cost information to management. In revenue-sensitive operations, on the other hand, they will essentially concentrate on the control of the sales volume, sales mix, profit margins, pricing of products/services, etc. These two different practical philosophies condition a great deal of the management accountant's outlook and day-to-day activities.

The *cost-oriented* approach is relevant to operations which have a large proportion of direct/variable/controllable costs and a low proportion of fixed/uncontrollable costs. Operations with such cost characteristics are to be found in most of the manufacturing, retail and construction and building industries, etc.

The *revenue-oriented* approach is relevant to business operations where direct/variable/controllable costs are low and fixed/uncontrollable costs constitute a high percentage of total cost. In such situations there is relatively little scope for cost manipulation or cost control. In order to secure adequate profitability we have to control first and foremost the revenue side of the business whilst, naturally, keeping an eye on operating costs.

Finally, management accounting in action is not about theoretical models or conceptual structures: it is primarily an activity relating to an actual business operation which, in all probability, is unique and very different from most other competitive operations in terms of capital employed, scale of operations, size of labour force, methods of production, style of management, etc. Management accounting methods which are eminently suitable in one business operation may, therefore, prove quite inappropriate in another.

■ SELF ASSESSMENT QUESTIONS

1 Explain what you understand by 'management accounting'.
2 Assess the role of the management accountant generally, and specifically in relation to the following functions of management:
(a) planning;
(b) decision making;
(c) controlling;
(d) evaluating.
3 Explain what you understand by the cost-oriented and revenue-oriented approaches to management accounting. Give examples of types of business operation where both of these approaches are relevant.

(Schiller International University)

4 Distinguish and define clearly the categories of costs that are appropriate for:
(a) planning;
(b) decision making;
(c) control.
Give marketing examples from each category.

(Institute of Marketing)

DISCUSSION PROBLEMS

1 Why is it important for a factory management accountant to be familiar with the actual operations of the company? How much time should he or she spend away from the office, on the shop floor?
2 What problems do you envisage in the evaluation of the performance of the following?
(a) chief buyer of a department store;
(b) training manager of a large bank with 100 branches;
(c) general manager of a light engineering company employing 500 people;
(d) sales manager of a trading company in charge of a sales force of 20 people.
3 As the role of the management accountant is to assist persons within the organization, does it mean that his or her work is not influenced by the external environment?

2 | Cost concepts and cost behaviour

The aim of this chapter is threefold. First, we need to provide definitions of various types of cost. Secondly, we will explore the behaviour of costs. Finally, we will explore the relevance of the various cost concepts to different kinds of situations.

■ FIXED, SEMI-FIXED AND VARIABLE COSTS

The distinction between fixed, semi-fixed and variable costs is of the utmost importance in the study of management accounting. Indeed, of all the cost concepts dealt with in this chapter, those relevant to cost behaviour (i.e. fixed, semi-fixed and variable costs) have probably the greatest impact on the day-to-day activities of the management accountant. Let us start with some preliminary definitions.

1 *Fixed costs* are those costs which do not respond to changes in the level of activity (i.e. output or volume of sales). Fixed costs are, in most kinds of business operations, expenses such as office salaries, rent, rates, depreciation of buildings, financial charges, etc. Whatever the level of activity, these costs tend to remain fixed.

2 *Semi-fixed costs* (sometimes also described as 'semi-variable'), are those which change in sympathy with, but not quite in proportion to, the level of activity. Examples of such costs are expenses such as telephone, stationery and repairs to plant and equipment. When the level of activity increases by 100 per cent, there will certainly be some increase in the cost of all these three items. We will make more frequent use of the telephone, but then whether we 'phone the supplier to order 100 or 200 hundred bags of cement makes no difference to the cost of the call. Similarly with a 100 per cent rise in the level of activity our plant and equipment will be subject to more intensive use. It is unlikely, however, that the resulting wear and tear will actually double.

3 *Variable costs* are those costs which move, for all practical purposes, in direct proportion to the level of activity. In the case of a trading organization, say a

retail shop, the cost of goods sold will vary in practically direct proportion to the sales volume and must, therefore, be regarded as a variable cost. In the case of a baker the cost of flour and any other appropriate ingredients will vary in proportion to the number of units (loaves) produced and will also be considered a variable cost. The cost of labour may be either fixed, semi-fixed or variable depending on the circumstances of the business operation concerned. Seasonal businesses, for instance hotels and travel agents, employ additional labour during the high season. As the cost involved is due to an increase in the level of activity it must be regarded as a variable cost.

EXAMPLE

John Smith has started in business as a manufacturer of men's shirts. During the first month of operations his fixed costs (rent, rates, insurance, office salaries, etc.) amounted to £20 000. Semi-fixed costs (stationery, repairs to plant and equipment, electricity and motoring expenses) amounted to £10 000. His total output of 10 000 shirts was sold at £8.00 per unit. The direct costs were as follows:
(a) cost of materials – £2.00 per unit;
(b) cost of labour – £1.00 per unit.

From this information we may prepare an estimate of the profitability of the operation at various possible levels of activity, as follows.

	Level of Activity (Units)			
	10 000	11 000	12 000	15 000
	£	£	£	£
Sales	80 000	88 000	96 000	120 000
Direct materials	20 000	22 000	24 000	30 000
Direct labour	10 000	11 000	12 000	15 000
Semi-fixed costs	10 000	10 500	11 000	12 500
Fixed costs	20 000	20 000	20 000	20 000
Total cost	60 000	63 500	67 000	77 500
Net profit	20 000	24 500	29 000	42 500
Total cost per unit	6.00	5.77	5.58	5.17
Net profit per unit	2.00	2.23	2.42	2.83
Selling price per unit	8.00	8.00	8.00	8.00

Notes on Profitability Statement
1   It should be noticed that the costs of materials and labour are wholly variable and change in direct proportion to the level of activity. → VC.
2   Semi-fixed costs show some, but not proportional, increase. Thus the increase in output from 10 000 to 15 000 units is one of 50 per cent. The resulting increase in semi-fixed costs (from £10 000 to £12 500) amounts to only 25 per cent.

3   Whatever the level of activity fixed costs are at the same level of £20 000.
4   When output is high, fixed costs are spread over a larger number of units. The higher the output, therefore, the lower the total cost per unit and the higher the net profit per unit.

When we speak of fixed, semi-fixed and variable costs we speak of such costs in the context of cost behaviour, i.e. how these costs respond to changes in the level of activity. Fig. 1 illustrates this aspect of cost behaviour. Fixed costs remain fixed whatever the level of activity. Variable costs are nil when activity is nil; they then increase in direct proportion to the level of activity. Some semi-fixed costs are incurred even when activity is nil; with every increase in the level of activity there is some, but not proportional, increase in semi-fixed costs.

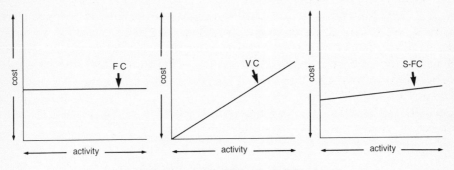

Fig. 1   *Fixed, variable and semi-fixed costs*

Fixed costs

Let us now take a closer look at fixed costs – their meaning and behaviour. Fixed costs may be divided into:
(a) *committed fixed costs* and
(b) *discretionary fixed costs*.
Committed fixed costs are costs which are unavoidable and must be incurred by the business in order to continue its operations. Examples of such costs are: rent, rates, salaries of indispensable employees as well as depreciation of lease, plant and equipment. An essential characteristic of committed fixed costs is their unavoidability.

Discretionary fixed costs are those which are avoidable, and given sufficient time (typically several months rather than years) may be altered – increased, decreased or discontinued by management action. Examples of such costs are: advertising and sales promotion, hire of plant and equipment, education and training programmes, etc. All these costs are fixed – once incurred – but they may be altered within a reasonably short period of time. Thus a company may discontinue certain forms of advertising; decide not to renew contracts for plant and equipment hire; disband its training department.

The distinction between committed and discretionary fixed costs is not always clear. An employee who was regarded as indispensable for several years may cease to be regarded as such: a committed cost would then become a discretionary fixed cost. A given piece of equipment may be hired for a period of five years by one company, whilst another company may be hiring the same equipment on a weekly basis. The cost would, in such circumstances, be committed for the former company and discretionary for the latter. Whilst the distinction is not always clear it is nevertheless valuable in that it is relevant to managerial decision making.

Fixed costs are not described as 'fixed' because they never change. During periods of inflation most fixed costs are, in fact, subject to periodical upward revision and will change quite frequently. When we say that a cost is fixed, what we do mean is that it does not change in response to changes in the level of activity.

Finally it should be appreciated that fixed costs are not fixed irrespective of the level of activity. A departmental store may be employing ten departmental managers – one in each department. Should the store open one or two more departments, or close a department or two, the number of its departmental managers will not remain constant. This particular cost is, therefore, fixed for a particular range of output called the *relevant range*. A large number of fixed costs are fixed for a particular range of business activity, and this is illustrated in Fig. 2.

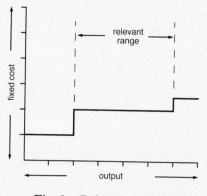

Fig. 2   *Relevant range*

Semi-fixed costs

We have already defined the semi-fixed cost as one which moves in the same direction, but not at the same rate, as the level of activity. The main reason for this pattern of cost behaviour is that semi-fixed costs are really a mixture of fully fixed and fully variable costs. It is for this reason that they are sometimes described as *mixed costs*. Where we do show a semi-fixed cost it is only because we have not taken the time or trouble to split it between the fully fixed and the fully variable elements.

Let us look at one or two examples. The quarterly telephone bill consists of two separate elements: the fixed quarterly rental plus the variable portion, dependent on actual use. The total quarterly charge is of a semi-fixed nature. The cost of labour is in many seasonal businesses a semi-fixed cost. A closer look at the cost of labour in any such business operation would disclose that whilst some of the employees are full-time and permanent, others are employed on a daily or weekly basis in response to the level of activity.

In most aspects of the management accountant's work it is inconvenient to have to deal with semi-fixed costs. It is certainly much easier if we can split the semi-fixed costs between the fully fixed and the fully variable elements. The fixed element we then add to the other fixed costs; and similarly the variable element we add to the other variable costs. Having done that, we now have just two cost categories: *fully fixed* and *fully variable costs*.

Two main methods may be used to split semi-fixed costs between the fixed and variable elements. These are the regression chart method and the high-low points method.

REGRESSION CHART

ABC Ltd is a seasonal business manufacturing a single product which is sold mainly during the six months to the end of September. Set out below is a table showing output and the resulting cost of electric power from January to August.

Month	Output Units	Electric Power-£
January	4 000	2 500
February	5 000	2 750
March	8 000	3 700
April	10 000	3 850
May	12 000	4 500
June	14 000	5 150
July	16 000	5 500
August	15 000	5 100

A regression chart is prepared as follows. We measure the semi-fixed cost of electric power vertically and the level of activity (number of units) horizontally. Having plotted all the points we draw a *line of best fit*. This should ideally cut through as many points as possible, leaving an equal number of odd points above and below.

From the regression chart in Fig. 3 it may be seen that the fully fixed element of the semi-fixed cost is £1 500. We may also see that a change in the output of 4 000 units causes a change in the variable element of £1 000. Dividing the latter by the former we obtain a variable element per unit of £0.25. It should be noted that our results are not affected by freak, untypical operating costs, as the points plotted above and below the line of best fit have no influence on the variable cost per unit or the fixed element.

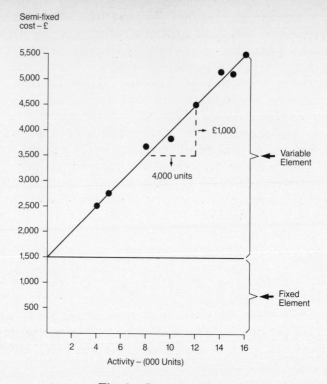

Fig. 3   *Regression chart*

HIGH-LOW POINTS

Under the high-low points method we pick a high and a low level of activity and ascertain the semi-fixed cost relevant to each. The difference between the two semi-fixed costs is then divided by the appropriate difference in the level of activity. An example will make this clear.

	Output Units	Semi-fixed Cost-£
High point – May	12 000	4 500
Low point – January	4 000	2 500
Change	8 000	2 000

A change in output of 8 000 units causes a change in the semi-fixed cost of £2 000. Again, by dividing the latter by the former we obtain a variable cost per unit of £0.25. Students will appreciate that the fixed element of the semi-fixed cost remains fixed. Consequently the change of £2 000 is a change in the variable element. Now that we know the variable element per unit we may calculate the fixed element. Thus:

	£
Total semi-fixed cost for July	5 500
Less variable element – 16 000 @ 25p	4 000
Therefore, fixed element	£1 500

Of course, had we chosen a high or low point which does not lie on the line of best fit our result would not have been exactly £0.25. The regression chart method is, therefore, more accurate than the high-low points method. When using the latter it is preferable to choose three or four sets of high and low points and average the results thus obtained for better precision. For instance if three calculations are made and our results are: £0.22, £0.26 and £0.27, we would assume that the variable cost per unit is (£0.22 + £0.26 + £0.27) ÷ 3 = £0.25.

Direct and indirect costs

The distinction between direct and indirect costs flows from the traceability of costs to units of output or departments. A cost may be direct in the sense that we can trace it to a department but not to a unit of output. In a department store we can trace the cost of shop assistants' wages to individual departments. It is impossible, however, to associate such costs with the sale of individual articles/items/products.

In all manufacturing operations the cost of materials is regarded as a direct cost. Administration, selling and distribution expenses, on the other hand, cannot be associated with individual products or even departments, and must be regarded as indirect costs. The cost of labour in manufacturing operations is commonly regarded as a direct cost, even though in practice it tends to be a fixed or semi-fixed cost, responding inadequately to changes in output.

In trading organizations the cost of goods sold is a direct cost: all expenditure under this heading is capable of being traced to individual items purchased. Also the cost is easily traceable to departments. The cost of labour is a direct cost in the sense that generally we may trace it to individual departments. Almost all other costs, e.g. rent, rates, office salaries, insurances, depreciation, etc. are clearly of an indirect nature.

Controllable and uncontrollable costs

The distinction between controllable and uncontrollable costs depends on management's ability to influence cost levels.

The cost of materials is generally a controllable cost. The cost of labour is to some extent controllable, but the degree of controllability will vary from one type of business operation to another. Many smaller businesses rely to a large extent on part-time and casual labour, and are able to maintain the total cost of labour at a predetermined level in relation to the level of activity. In other situations we frequently see an almost fixed labour force being employed over long periods irrespective of fluctuations in output. Where that is so, management's ability to control this cost of labour is severely limited.

Students should appreciate that the controllability of costs depends on the level of authority. From the marketing manager's point of view the cost of labour in his or her department may be fixed and uncontrollable. During a slack period, however, the manager may be required by the managing director to reduce the sales force, merchandisers, etc: a cost previously regarded as uncontrollable is now, as a result of management action at a higher level, quite controllable.

The concepts of controllable and uncontrollable costs are useful in many areas of management accounting, and especially in budgeting where the element of executive responsibility is clearly very prominent.

Sunk costs

Reference is sometimes made to sunk costs. A sunk cost is one which has already been incurred. It is important to realize that such costs cannot have any relevance to management decisions.

Many management decisions relate to choice between alternative courses of action. For instance: should certain plant and equipment be purchased or hired – and if so, should it be hired on a monthly, quarterly or other basis; should a particular product/part be manufactured internally or purchased outside; should one of the branches be closed during a slack period? In all such decisions sunk costs, because they have already been incurred, will not change whichever alternative course of action is decided upon.

A typical example of a sunk cost is the cost of plant and equipment. All other costs *already incurred* – including wages, salaries, advertising, etc. – are also sunk costs and therefore irrelevant in management decision making.

Estimated, budgeted and standard costs

When we estimate we predict future events, occurrences or trends. For example, we may say: 'the cost of materials was £10 per unit last year, it is £11 this year and so it will probably be £12 next year'. When we make an estimate like this we are projecting, in a detached and indifferent manner, an existing trend into the future.

When we budget, our intention comes into play. And so we may say: 'the cost of material was £10 per unit last year, it is costing us £11 per unit this year, but we must make every effort to ensure we don't pay more than £11.50 per unit next year'. The £12 in the first example is an estimated cost; the £11.50 in the second a budgeted cost. When we budget, we are no longer detached or indifferent. A budgeted cost is therefore a *normative cost*, i.e. one which reflects management's intention with regard to what should or ought to take place in the future.

Both budgeted and standard costs are normative costs in that they are pre-determined in relation to management plans. Standard costs, however, are different from budgeted costs in that they are normally built up from a great deal of detail. Thus the standard cost of a pair of men's shoes would be built up by reference to the standard quantity of the required materials, standard prices to be paid for such materials, standard direct cost of labour and, possibly, a standard rate of overhead in respect of administration, selling and distribution expenses. On the other hand, the cost of press or television advertising would be expressed as a budgeted figure of £X. It should just be added that, in practice, the terms 'budgeted cost' and 'standard cost' are sometimes regarded as interchangeable.

Average costs and marginal costs

Average cost may be defined as total cost divided by the number of units produced. Marginal cost, on the other hand, is the increase in total cost resulting from one more unit (or batch of units) being produced. Whilst, therefore, average cost is fully inclusive (of both fixed and variable costs), marginal cost reflects the changes occurring in the variable portion of the total cost per unit.

A simple example will make these definitions clear. A company produces product 'A' and sells all the output at £10.00 per unit. Fixed costs amount to £4 000 and variable costs are incurred at the rate of £5.00 per unit.

No. of Units	1 000	1 001	1 002	1 003
	£	£	£	£
Sales Volume	10 000	10 010	10 020	10 030
Fixed Costs	4 000	4 000	4 000	4 000
Variable Costs	5 000	5 005	5 010	5 015
Total Cost	9 000	9 005	9 010	9 015
Net Profit	1 000	1 005	1 010	1 015

When 1 000 units are produced average cost is (£9 000 ÷ 1 000) = £9.00. An increase in output from 1 000 to 1 001 units increases total cost by £5.00 and total revenue (sales volume) by £10.00. The £5.00 increase in the variable element of total cost is described as *marginal cost* whilst the £10.00 increase in total revenue is described as *marginal revenue*. Every increase in output will decrease the total cost per unit; marginal cost will, however, tend to remain constant at £5.00.

The distinction between average cost and marginal cost is of paramount importance. Whilst in some situations we should look at average costs, in other situations it is right to think in terms of marginal costs. As a general rule, in long-term strategic situations, we use the average cost concept; and the reason for this approach is that over a long period we must cover all costs – both variable and fixed. In the short term fixed costs remain fixed and, in such circumstances, it is as well to keep the fixed costs in the background and concentrate on marginal costs only.

Outlay costs and opportunity costs

An outlay cost is the actual financial expenditure which is recorded in the accounting records. All costs which have already been incurred are outlay costs, and these are the costs which we see recorded in the books of every business.

An opportunity cost, on the other hand, is the benefit lost by taking one course of action rather than another. The concept of opportunity cost is not easy to comprehend, even though opportunity costs are present in all business decisions.

Let us assume that a trading organization has accumulated cash of £100 000, which is not currently needed for operational purposes. Several immediate opportunities may present themselves for investing this cash. For instance, it may be possible to:

(a) extend existing premises which, it is estimated, would contribute an additional £15 000 to total company cash resources;

(b) invest the cash in securities which would produce additional cash of £10 000;

(c) refurbish and redecorate all existing selling outlets, which would improve the image of the organisation, but it is estimated would add not more than £5 000 to company cash resources.

If it is decided to extend the existing premises then, clearly, the benefit of the additional cash from the enlarged premises will be secured by sacrificing the potential cash from the possible investment in securities. It should be remembered that where several opportunities exist, the opportunity cost is the contribution of the most profitable venture foregone by using the resources for some other purpose. In the present example, therefore, the benefit of the additional cash of £15 000 is secured by sacrificing the £10 000 cash from investing in securities.

■ SELF ASSESSMENT QUESTIONS

1 Distinguish clearly between:
   (a) fixed and variable costs;
   (b) direct and indirect costs;
   (c) controllable and uncontrollable costs;
   (d) estimated and budgeted costs;
   (e) average and marginal costs.

2 The following two quotations are taken from a management accounting text:

'In the long run all costs are variable because an increase in production leads to lower costs.'

'A marginal cost approach must be the right one because all we need to monitor are variable costs as the fixed costs can look after themselves.'

You are required to make a critical examination of both of the above quotations.

(Association of Business Executives)

3 What major differences exist in applying financial analysis to short-run issues as opposed to long-run issues?

(Institute of Marketing)

4 Explain why sunk costs are irrelevant to management decisions.

5 (a) Complete the following table:

Output (Units)	Fixed Cost	Variable Cost	Total Cost	Sales Revenue	Profit (Loss)
	£	£	£	£	£
1 000	10 000	12 000	22 000	20 000	(2 000)
1 200	10 000	14 400	24 400	24 000	(400)
1 400	10 000	16 800	26 800	28 000	1 200
1 600	10 000	19 200	29 200	32 000	2 800
1 800					
2 000					

(b) Calculate the following:
   (i) marginal cost;
   (ii) marginal revenue.
(c) Calculate the average cost per unit of output for the following levels of activity:
   (i)   1 000 units;
   (ii) 1 400 units;
   (iii) 1 800 units.

6 Set out below is the cost of electric power of a seasonal business.

Month	Output (Units)	Electric Power
		£
April	6 000	5 200
May	8 000	5 600
June	10 000	6 000
July	12 000	6 640
August	14 000	6 800
September	16 000	7 200
October	18 000	7 300
November	20 000	8 000

You are required to split the semi-fixed cost of electric power into its fully fixed and fully variable elements by means of:
(a) regression chart method;
(b) high-low points method.

7 Given below are particulars of monthly labour costs and the numbers of transactions (bookings) of a travel agent.

Month	No of trans-actions	Cost of labour £
January	400	5 600
February	600	6 400
March	800	7 600
April	1 300	9 200
May	1 500	10 000
June	700	6 100
July	500	6 000

You are required to prepare a regression chart and calculate the fixed and variable elements of the total cost of labour. Check the accuracy of your calculations by means of the high-low points method.

3 Break-even analysis

■ THE BREAK-EVEN POINT

The break-even point denotes a situation where _total sales are equal to the total cost_ of running a business; in other words, it is a state of affairs or condition when there is no net profit and no net loss. Let us start with a simple example.

EXAMPLE

A trading company sells a single product, Product A. Its fixed costs are £4 500 per month and monthly sales vary from 1 000 to 2 000 units of A. The variable cost is £2.00 and the selling price £5.00 per unit. Set out below is a table showing the sales, costs, profits and losses for each possible monthly level of activity.

Units Sold	Fixed Cost £	Variable Cost £	Total Cost £	Sales Revenue £	Profit (Loss) £
1 000	4 500	2 000	6 500	5 000	(1 500)
1 100	4 500	2 200	6 700	5 500	(1 200)
1 200	4 500	2 400	6 900	6 000	(900)
1 300	4 500	2 600	7 100	6 500	(600)
1 400	4 500	2 800	7 300	7 000	(300)
1 500	4 500	3 000	7 500	7 500	—
1 600	4 500	3 200	7 700	8 000	300
1 700	4 500	3 400	7 900	8 500	600
1 800	4 500	3 600	8 100	9 000	900
1 900	4 500	3 800	8 300	9 500	1 200
2 000	4 500	4 000	8 500	10 000	1 500

Three main conclusions may be drawn from our table:

1 Every change in the number of units sold causes a proportional change in:
(a) sales revenue;
(b) variable cost.
2 Total cost, being a mixture of fixed costs and variable costs, moves in sympathy with but not in proportion to the number of units sold.
3 The break-even point is reached when the company sells 1 500 units of A. At this level of activity *total cost is equal to total sales volume.*

A simple formula for calculating the break-even point in terms of units of output or sales is:

$$\frac{\text{Fixed Costs}}{\text{Unit Price} - \text{Variable Cost per Unit}} = \text{BEP}$$

We may apply the formula to our example, as follows:

$$\frac{£4\ 500.00}{(£5.00 - £2.00) = £3.00} = 1\ 500 \ (\text{Units of Product A})$$

Contribution and P/V ratio

Contribution may be defined as the excess of sales over variable cost. It is a surplus which, in the first instance, is available to cover fixed costs. When fixed costs have been covered any further contribution is available as net profit.

The profit to volume ratio (P/V ratio) is closely related to the concept of contribution. It is a percentile expression of contribution in relation to sales volume.

Let us re-write the table in our last example to make these two new concepts clear.

Units Sold	Sales Revenue £	Variable Cost £	Contribution £	
1 000	5 000	2 000	3 000	
1 100	5 500	2 200	3 300	
1 200	6 000	2 400	3 600	
1 300	6 500	2 600	3 900	
1 400	7 000	2 800	4 200	
1 500	7 500	3 000	4 500	→ Equal to Fixed Costs
1 600	8 000	3 200	4 800	
1 700	8 500	3 400	5 100	
1 800	9 000	3 600	5 400	
1 900	9 500	3 800	5 700	
2 000	10 000	4 000	6 000	

A closer look at the above table will enable us to draw the following conclusions:
(a) Every increase of 100 units sold adds £300 to total contribution.
(b) When the company sells 1 500 units the total contribution is £4 500, which is equal to fixed costs. At this level of activity there is no profit and no loss and, consequently, the break-even point is reached.
(c) Contribution represents a constant percentage of the sales volume. Whatever the number of units sold it is always 60 per cent of the sales revenue. We would say, therefore, that the company has a P/V ratio of 60 per cent.

We have already defined the break-even point as a situation where sales revenue is equal to total cost. We may now suggest a second definition and say that *the break-even point is a situation where contribution is equal to fixed costs*. This is further illustrated by the calculations given below.

Units Sold	1 400	1 500	1 600
	£	£	£
Sales Revenue	7 000	7 500	8 000
less Variable Costs	2 800	3 000	3 200
Contribution	4 200	4 500	4 800
less Fixed Costs	4 500	4 500	4 500
N. Profit, (N. Loss)	(300)	—	300

Also we may define net profit as the excess of contribution over fixed costs; and, conversely, define net loss as the excess of fixed costs over contribution. It will be realised that it is now possible to simplify the formula for the break-even point, and re-write it as follows:

$$\frac{\text{Fixed Costs}}{\text{Contribution per Unit}} = \text{BEP}$$

Fig. 4 illustrates the relationship between sales, variable costs, contribution and the resulting net profit for 2 000 units of the product.

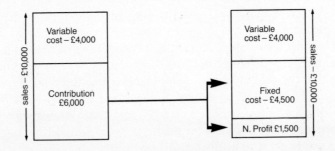

Fig. 4 *The concept of contribution*

Contribution as a percentage of the sales volume, i.e. the P/V ratio, will vary considerably from one type of business operation to another. Where variable costs are low – as in the case of theatres, cinemas, public transport, etc. – the P/V ratio may sometimes be as high as 90 per cent. Where, on the other hand, a business operates a high level of variable costs – which applies to most forms of retail distribution, construction and building industries – the P/V ratio will, by definition, be low.

From the dynamic point of view a high P/V ratio is of great importance. In the short run fixed costs are fixed; and where the P/V ratio is high, changes in the level of activity will have a powerful effect on the profitability of the business. This is illustrated below by reference to two businesses – A and B. Business A operates at a high level of variable costs, and its P/V ratio is 30 per cent. Business B has a low level of variable costs and its P/V ratio is 70 per cent. Both businesses have a normal sales volume of £100 000 per month. One month, however, both A and B have an increase of 10 per cent in the volume of sales revenue.

	Business A		Business B	
	Normal Sales Vol.	Increased Sales Vol.	Normal Sales Vol.	Increased Sales Vol.
	£	£	£	£
Sales Revenue	100 000	110 000	100 000	110 000
less Variable Costs	70 000	77 000	30 000	33 000
Contribution	30 000	33 000	70 000	77 000
less Fixed Costs	20 000	20 000	60 000	60 000
Net Profit	10 000	13 000	10 000	17 000

From the above calculation it is clear that a high P/V ratio produces a relatively strong impact on net profit in conditions of rising sales revenues. In the present example the 10 per cent increase in the sales revenue of A has increased the net profit by 30 per cent. The same rise in the sales revenue of B has increased its net profit by 70 per cent.

It should be appreciated, however, that when sales volumes are falling it is the business with a high percentage of fixed costs that suffers more. Our conclusion is, therefore, that the cost structure of a business (i.e. the relative proportions of fixed and variable costs) is a strong determinant of *profit stability*. Business operations with a high percentage of variable costs tend to enjoy a relatively high degree of profit stability. Conversely, business operations with a high percentage of fixed costs tend to suffer from profit instability.

■ BREAK-EVEN CHARTS

The main purpose of a break-even chart is to show the profit or loss that will be made at various levels of activity. The term 'break-even chart' is rather unfortunate in that it stresses just one particular level of activity, i.e. that which ensures the equality of total cost and total sales revenue.

There are very many different kinds of break-even charts that may be prepared; and several examples – covering the main possibilities – will be illustrated in this chapter. Also, students should appreciate that it is possible to prepare a break-even chart in respect of a past period or for a given future period. In the former case, we would take the necessary information from the already available Profit & Loss A/c. In the latter case, we would base the break-even chart on budgeted sales, costs, etc. Finally, the period covered by a break-even chart may be, at least in theory, anything from one day to one year. In practice, monthly, quarterly and annual break-even charts are more common.

Basic break-even chart

John Smith is a trader. His monthly fixed costs amount to £30 000. He sells a single product at £10.00 per unit and the variable cost per unit (i.e. price paid to the manufacturer) is £4.00. During May 19.., Smith sold 10 000 units. You are asked to prepare his break-even chart.

SOLUTION
Students should remember that they need three items of information to prepare a break-even chart. These are:
1   Total sales;
2   Total fixed cost;
3   Total variable cost.

In this case the relevant figures are:

1   Total sales – 10 000 @ £10.00   £100 000
2   Total fixed cost – given   £ 30 000
3   Total variable cost – 10 000 @ £4.00   £ 40 000

Our procedure in preparing a break-even chart is as follows. We represent fixed costs by a straight line parallel to the horizontal axis. In order to show the total cost, variable costs are then placed on top of the fixed costs. Thus when activity is nil total cost is £30 000 (when only fixed costs are incurred); when 10 000 units are sold total cost is (fixed cost – £30 000 plus variable cost – £40 000) £70 000. The break-even point is indicated by the intersection of the sales and total cost lines. The break-even chart is shown in Fig. 5.

From the break-even chart we may see that the break-even point is reached when 5 000 units are sold. The margin of safety represents the range of activity

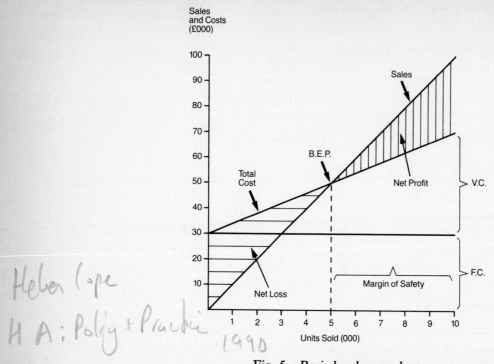

Fig. 5   *Basic break-even chart*

over which some profit is made. John Smith will be 'safe' if he sells each month at least 5 000 units, as anything over and above this level of activity will result in net profit.

Let us now check the accuracy of the break-even point by means of the formula with which we are already familiar.

	£	%
Selling Price per Unit	10.00	100.0
less Variable Cost per Unit	4.00	40.0
Contribution and P/V Ratio	£ 6.00	60.0 %

Hence:
$$\frac{\text{Fixed Costs} - £30\,000}{\text{Contribution per Unit} - £6.00} = 5\,000 \text{ (units)}$$

As the break-even point is 5 000 units and the P/V ratio 60 per cent, we know that 60 per cent of any additional sales revenue over and above the break-even point will go into net profit. Let us assume that one month Smith sells 7 000 units. His net profit will be as follows.

	£
Sales: 7 000 units @ £10.00	70 000
less: Sales at BEP – 5 000 @ £10.00	50 000
Sales above the BEP	20 000
Of which 60 per cent, i.e. Net Profit	£12 000

The £12 000 net profit may be checked as follows:

	£	£
Sales		70 000
less Fixed costs	£30 000	
Variable costs – 7 000 @ £4.00	28 000	58 000
Net Profit		£12 000

Contribution break-even chart

The contribution break-even chart serves basically the same purpose as any other break-even chart. Its added advantage, however, is that it highlights the

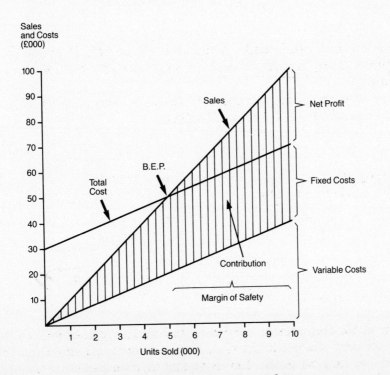

Fig. 6 *Contribution break-even chart*

importance of contribution, which is not readily apparent in the basic break-even chart in Fig. 5.

The contribution break-even chart in Fig. 6 is based on John Smith's business. Students will note that the costs are shown differently: we have drawn the variable cost line first and then added the fixed costs. The shaded area lying between the sales line and variable cost line represents total contribution. It should be noticed that at the break-even point here contribution is equal to fixed costs.

Pricing break-even chart

A pricing break-even chart is a useful aid in price level decisions. Essentially it indicates what profit/loss will result from various possible price levels.

In the break-even chart in Fig. 7 we project three possible price levels: £8.00, £9.00 and £10.00. Each price level results in a different volume of sales, net profit, break-even point and margin of safety.

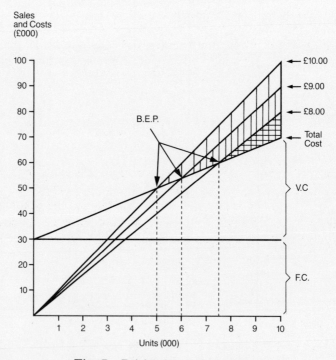

Fig. 7   *Pricing break-even chart*

In this particular case we have assumed that neither fixed costs nor variable cost per unit are controllable; and we are manipulating the price level to achieve the most appropriate net profit. Students will appreciate that, sometimes, the price per unit must be regarded as fixed; and we may then try to manipulate the variable cost per unit to secure the appropriate amount of net profit.

Profit-volume graph

Essentially the profit-volume graph is a device similar to the break-even chart, but the two differ in the method of construction. Let us take one example.

A company's Profit and Loss A/c shows in respect of the last quarter the following: (a) sales – £200 000; (b) fixed costs – £80 000; (c) variable costs – £80 000 and (d) net profit of £40 000.

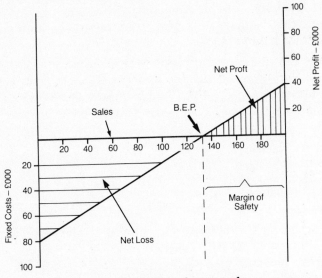

Fig. 8 *Profit-volume graph*

The method of preparation is as follows. The left-hand side vertical axis measures fixed costs. The vertical axis on the right-hand side measures net profit. A straight line from total fixed costs (£80 000) to the point denoting net profit (£40 000) cuts the sales line at the break-even point, which is approximately £130 000. If we need the exact break-even point we may resort to our formula as shown below.

	£	%
Sales	200 000	100.0
less Variable Costs	80 000	40.0
Contribution and P/V Ratio	£120 000	60.0 %

As we do not know what the business here is producing or selling, we assume for the purposes of our calculations that the 'unit' is £1.00 of sales revenue. Clearly then every £1 of sales revenue brings a contribution of £0.60. Hence:

$$\frac{\text{Fixed Costs} - \pounds80\,000}{\text{Contribution per unit} - \pounds0.60} = 133,333^{\cdot}$$

Our precise break-even point is, therefore, 133,333· assumed 'units' of £1.00 of sales revenue, i.e. £133,333·.

Profit-volume graph – alternative version

There is another type of profit-volume graph, which is particularly useful in situations where the only information available consists of periodical sales volumes and net profit or net loss – that is in situations where total cost is not divided into its fixed and variable elements.

Let us assume that we have been given the following information extracted from the books of a seasonal business.

Month	Sales Revenue £	Net Profit (Net Loss) £
January	200 000	(100 000)
February	600 000	100 000
March	700 000	200 000
April	800 000	200 000
May	900 000	220 000
June	1 000 000	300 000

The procedure here is as follows. The monthly sales volume is measured horizontally; and the vertical axis is used to measure the monthly net profit and monthly net loss. The line of best fit indicates that the break-even point is reached when monthly sales amount to £400 000.

When sales are nil the monthly net loss amounts to £200 000, and this indicates that fixed costs are incurred at the rate of £200 000 per month. Clearly, when sales are nil no variable costs are incurred and the £200 000 must necessarily represent fixed costs.

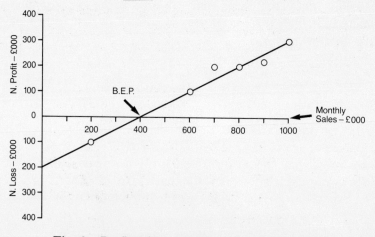

Fig. 9   *Profit-volume graph – alternative version*

We may now calculate the percentage of fixed costs and the P/V ratio. If we take the figures for June:

		£
Sales		1 000 000
less Fixed Costs	200 000	
Net Profit	300 000	500 000
Therefore, Variable Costs		£ 500 000

Our contribution is therefore (£1 000 000 − £500 000) £500 000, which indicates a P/V ratio of 50 per cent.

Limitations of break-even charts

Break-even charts have many important advantages: they are simple in construction, easy to understand and give a great deal of insight into profitability. They do, however, have some limitations, and it is important that these should be appreciated.

The first limitation relates to the *time factor*. During inflationary periods there is often a significant upward trend in all operating costs. As, in such circumstances, we cannot be too sure about future cost levels, it is not safe to prepare a break-even chart for a period longer than one year.

Our second problem is *linearity*. When we draw a straight line to represent the sales volume, we do this on the assumption that whatever the physical volume the price per unit is constant. This, in practice, is not always so. Frequently it is necessary to offer discounts to increase the number of units sold. Similar considerations apply to the cost of sales: with larger sales volumes our volume of purchases will necessarily increase which, in turn, may enable us to secure discounts from our suppliers.

Thirdly, we have the problem of *sales mix* (i.e. percentage composition of total sales). A business may be selling a number of different products or operating several different departments, each of which has a different cost structure in terms of fixed and variable costs. Let us assume that a business operates three departments as shown below.

	Sales £000	%	V'ble Costs £000	%	Contribution £000	%
Department A	500	50.0	400	80.0	100	20.0
Department B	300	30.0	180	60.0	120	40.0
Department C	200	20.0	40	40.0	160	60.0
Total	1 000	100.0	620	62.0	380	38.0
less Fixed Operating Expenses					180	18.0
Net Profit					200	20.0

Quite obviously if there is a 10 per cent increase in sales revenue, then this does not necessarily imply a 10 per cent increase in each department. If most of the increase is secured in Department C – where variable costs are low – the effect will be to reduce the overall variable cost and improve the P/V ratio for the business as a whole. The impact on net profit will be greater than would have been expected from the P/V ratio before the increase in sales. The reverse will apply if most of the overall 10 per cent increase in revenue were attributable to Department A where variable costs are high and the departmental P/V ratio is low. When preparing break-even charts we assume that the sales mix will remain constant, just as we assume a linear relationship in the case of total sales volume and cost of sales. Having prepared the break-even chart, however, we should remember such assumptions. If subsequently there is a significant change in either the sales mix or purchase/selling prices, the break-even chart should be re-drawn accordingly.

Finally we have the problem of *common costs*. Common costs are fixed costs which are incurred for the benefit of the business as a whole and not for the benefit of any one particular department. Examples of common costs are: head office salaries, sales promotion and advertising, financial charges, rates, insurance of buildings, etc.

Common costs do not present a problem in the preparation of a break-even chart for a business as a whole. When, however, it is necessary to prepare a break-even chart for a particular department the problem of common costs presents itself immediately. There are, essentially, two possibilities. The first possible solution is to apportion the fixed costs on some fair basis, i.e. split the total common costs as between the departments concerned. The second possibility is to ignore the common costs and base the break-even chart on departmental costs only. With the second solution, the profit wedge will represent 'departmental profit' rather than net profit; the loss wedge will similarly represent 'departmental loss' rather than net loss.

■ SELF ASSESSMENT QUESTIONS

1 The standard costs of producing and selling a single product are as follows:

Material per Unit	£10
Labour per Unit	£ 7
Variable Overheads	£ 3
Fixed Overheads	£15
Standard Cost per Unit	£35

The fixed overhead per unit is based on a budget of £4500 recovered over the maximum capacity of 300 units.

The management accountant points out that as the expected selling price is £40 the standard profit per unit is £5 per unit.

Required:
(a) How many units would have to be produced and sold to make a profit of £500?
(b) How many units would have to be produced and sold to break even?
(c) What is the P/V ratio?
(d) How many units would be required to break even if the fixed cost doubled and the selling price also doubled?
(e) What do you understand by the Margin of Safety?

(Association of Business Executives)

2 'The City Tower' is a travel agency which, amongst others, specializes in running one-day sight-seeing tours for foreign tourists. The following information is available:
(a) coach capacity – 30 passengers;
(b) price charged – £10.00 per passenger;
(c) daily cost of coach hire – £60.00;
(d) other costs, e.g. admission tickets, information sheets, leaflets, etc. amount to £4.00 per passenger.

You are required to:
(i) prepare a break-even chart for the tour;
(ii) ascertain the break-even point and the margin of safety.

3 As the Managing Director of Veasy Ltd you have been provided with the following information for the quarter ended 31 December 1985.

		£
Sales (225 000 units)		180 000
Variable Costs:		
Materials	65 000	
Production Labour	56 000	
Production Overhead	9 500	
Sales Commission	4 500	
		135 000
Fixed Costs:		
Production	7 000	
Sales	5 000	
		12 000
Total Costs		147 000
Net Profit		33 000

Required:
(a) A calculation of the break-even point for the quarter ended 31 December 1985.
(b) A calculation of the additional sales required to produce the same profit for the first quarter of 1986 that was achieved for the last quarter of 1985 given that a pay increase of 10% for productive labour is to take effect on 1 January 1986. No increase in selling prices is planned.

(c) A graph showing the BEP in (a) and the BEP in (b).
(d) Brief comments on the limitations of break-even analysis.

(Association of Business Executives)

4   John Smith, a sole trader, is considering selling Product 'A'. The variable cost (i.e. price paid to the manufacturer) would be £3.00 per unit and the fixed costs entailed by the operation would amount to £40 000 per annum. He reckons he could sell 10 000 units of 'A' per annum at a price of £8–£10. You are required to prepare a pricing break-even chart for Smith to show how much profit he would make on the 10 000 units at a price of: (a) £8.00; (b) £9.00 and (c) £10.00. Also calculate the margin of safety for each of the three possible price levels.

(Schiller International University)

5   From the following information you are required,
(a) to calculate the unit selling price,
(b) prepare the break-even chart,
(c) calculate the total profit, and
(d) calculate the profit if the cost of ingredients rises by 10% and the selling price was reduced by 10%.

Autumn Products operates on a seasonal basis preparing and selling Christmas food hampers. The company's fixed costs amount to £10 000. The cost of ingredients is £80 per hamper. Each hamper costs £5 and takes 2 hours at £2.50 per hour to pack and decorate. The company anticipates selling 1 000 hampers at a unit selling price of total cost plus 40% mark up.

(Institute of Marketing)

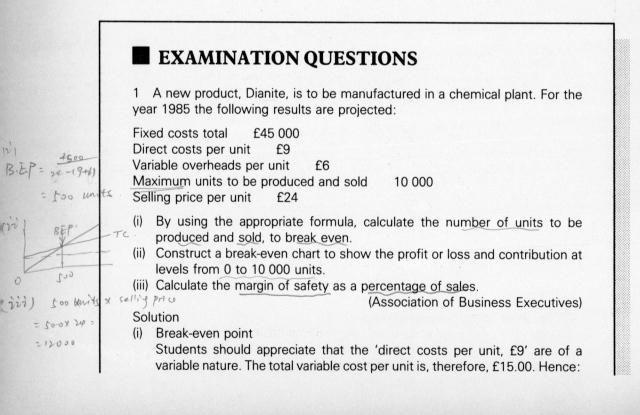

■ EXAMINATION QUESTIONS

1   A new product, Dianite, is to be manufactured in a chemical plant. For the year 1985 the following results are projected:

Fixed costs total	£45 000
Direct costs per unit	£9
Variable overheads per unit	£6
Maximum units to be produced and sold	10 000
Selling price per unit	£24

(i)   By using the appropriate formula, calculate the number of units to be produced and sold, to break even.
(ii) Construct a break-even chart to show the profit or loss and contribution at levels from 0 to 10 000 units.
(iii) Calculate the margin of safety as a percentage of sales.

(Association of Business Executives)

Solution
(i)   Break-even point
      Students should appreciate that the 'direct costs per unit, £9' are of a variable nature. The total variable cost per unit is, therefore, £15.00. Hence:

	£
Selling Price per Unit	24.00
less Variable Costs	15.00
Contribution	9.00

$$\frac{\text{Fixed Costs} - £45\,000}{\text{Contribution/Unit} - £9} = \underline{5\,000 \text{ units}}$$

(ii) Break-even chart

As the break-even chart is to show the contribution over the whole range of output, what is required here is a contribution break-even chart, such as shown in Fig. 10.

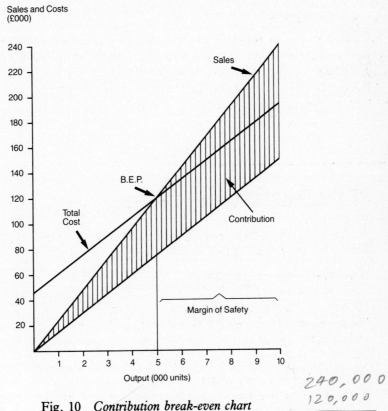

Fig. 10 *Contribution break-even chart*

240,000
120,000
―――――
120,000
5,000

(iii) Margin of Safety

As 5 000 units need to be produced and sold to break even, in terms of the sales revenue this is equivalent to (5 000 × £24) £120 000, which means that the margin of safety is equal to 50 per cent.

2 *The Broomhill Manufacturing Company* has the following revenue and cost characteristics for its only product:

Selling price per unit	£6.00
Variable cost per unit	£4.20
Annual fixed costs	£360 000
Annual volume	270 000 units

Required:
(a) Determine the following:
   (i) contribution to sales ratio;
   (ii) contribution margin per unit;
   (iii) break-even point in units and in £s;
   (iv) net profit at current operating level;
   (v) margin of safety.
(b) For each of the following *independent* cases, determine the new contribution to sales ratio, break-even point in £s, and net profit.
(i) Decrease in variable costs of £0.60 per unit and 20% increase in selling price;
(ii) 20% decrease in fixed costs and 20% increase in variable costs.

(Institute of Marketing)

Solution

Part (a)
(i) Contribution to Sales Ratio
   (Students should realize that this is the same as the P/V ratio.)

	£	%
Selling Price per Unit	6.00	100.0
less Variable Cost	4.20	70.0
Contribution and P/V Ratio	1.80	30.0

(ii) Contribution Margin per Unit
   This has already been calculated in (i) above.
(iii) Break-even point

$$\frac{\text{Fixed Costs} \quad £360\,000}{\text{Contribution/Unit} \quad £1.80} = 200\,000 \text{ units}$$

In terms of sales revenue the break-even point is (200 000 × £6.00) £1 200 000.

(iv) Net Profit

	£000	£000
Sales (270 000 units @ £6.00)		1 620
less Fixed costs	360	
Variable Costs		
(270 000 units @ £4.20)	1 134	1 494
Net Profit		126

(v) Margin of Safety

	Units (000)	%
Current Sales Volume	270	100.0
less Sales Volume at break-even point	200	74.1
Margin of Safety	70	25.9

Part (b)
(i) Effect on P/V Ratio, Break-even Point and Net Profit

	£	%
Selling Price (£6.00 + £1.20)	7.20	100.0
less Variable Cost (£4.20 − £0.60)	3.60	50.0
Contribution and P/V Ratio	3.60	50.0

$$\frac{\text{Fixed Costs} \quad £360\,000}{\text{Contribution/Unit} \quad £3.60} = \underline{100\,000 \text{ units}}$$

In terms of sales revenue this is equal to £720 000.

	£000	£000
Sales (270 000 @ £7.20)		1 944
less Fixed Costs	360	
Variable Costs (270 000 @ £3.60)	972	1 332
Net Profit		612

(ii) Effect on P/V Ratio, Break-even Point and Net Profit

	£	%
Selling Price	6.00	100.0
less Variable Cost (£4.20 + £0.84)	5.04	84.0
Contribution and P/V Ratio	0.96	16.0

$$\frac{\text{Fixed Costs (£360\,000 − £72\,000)} \quad £288\,000}{\text{Contribution/Unit (£6.00 − £5.04)} \quad £0.96} = \underline{300\,000 \text{ units}}$$

In terms of sales revenue, this is equal to £1 800 000.

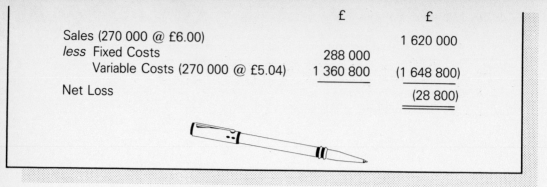

	£	£
Sales (270 000 @ £6.00)		1 620 000
less Fixed Costs	288 000	
Variable Costs (270 000 @ £5.04)	1 360 800	(1 648 800)
Net Loss		(28 800)

4 Marginal costing

Marginal costing is not so much a system of cost or management accounting like, for instance, budgetary control, but rather *a technique for short-run decision making.*

When we look at the nature of business decisions it is apparent that they have two main characteristics. First, most business decisions relate to a *relatively short period of time.* As already mentioned in Chapter 2, pricing decisions as well as decisions relating to possible closure of a department, size of output, hire of plant and equipment – all tend to relate to what is about to happen this week, this month or in the otherwise near future. Over a short period of one week, one month, etc. the fixed costs of the business will tend to remain unchanged. Therefore, whether we close down a department or purchase rather than hire some equipment should not, in any way, be affected by the fixed costs of the business. In all such decisions we concentrate on the variable elements relevant to each decision, i.e. sales volume and variable cost; and assume that fixed costs are irrelevant and should not have any bearing on the decision concerned.

Secondly, *all decisions relate to a choice between alternative courses of action.* Here it should be remembered that costs already incurred cannot possibly have any bearing on future courses of action. Past costs are, therefore, irrelevant costs and should not be allowed to influence current or future business decisions.

■ MARGINAL COSTING PHILOSOPHY

We may, therefore, summarize the philosophy of marginal costing as follows. Marginal costing entails:

1 The segregation of all costs into fixed and variable costs.
2 The assumption that, in the short term, all fixed costs will remain fixed and should consequently be kept in the background.

3   The recognition that variable costs are the only relevant costs in short-run decision making.

In absorption costing (see Chapter 5) we adopt the full-cost approach: we take into account both fixed and variable costs in order to arrive at the total cost of each department and each product. This enables the accountant to arrive at the net profit of each department and product.

In marginal costing we concentrate on sales, variable costs and the resulting contribution. As, in the short run, fixed costs remain fixed, *the size of the contribution is the most important criterion in all short-run decision making*.

The remainder of the present chapter will now be devoted to examples and illustrations of marginal costing.

■ CLOSURE OF DEPARTMENT

A business consists of three departments, A, B and C, and the following profit statement has been prepared to show the contribution of each department to overall profits.

	Dept A £000	Dept B £000	Dept C £000	Total £000
Sales	500	300	200	1 000
Direct Materials	150	75	75	300
Direct Labour	125	85	90	300
Direct Expenses	25	10	15	50
Apportioned Fixed Costs	120	80	50	250
Total Cost	420	250	230	900
Net Profit (Net Loss)	80	50	(30)	100

You are required to rewrite the above statement in the form of a Contribution Profit and Loss Account, and suggest whether, in view of the poor results in Department C, management should consider its closure. For the purpose of your answer assume that the closure of Department C would not have any effect on the fixed costs of the business.

SOLUTION

Contribution Profit and Loss Account for ...

	Dept A	Dept B	Dept C	Total
	£000	£000	£000	£000
Sales	500	300	200	1 000
less Variable Costs:				
Direct Materials	150	75	75	300
Direct Labour	125	85	90	300
Direct Expenses	25	10	15	50
	300	170	180	650
Contribution	200	130	20	350
less Fixed Costs				250
Net Profit				100

It will be observed that the important features of the contribution profit and loss account are:
(a) the emphasis on the contribution made by each department (or product), and
(b) the non-apportionment of fixed costs.

If we were to close Department C the business would be worse off to the extent of £20 000. Another way of looking at the consequences of the closure of Department C is as follows:

Gain: i.e. saving of Variable Costs	£	£
Direct Materials	75 000	
Direct Labour	90 000	
Direct Expenses	15 000	180 000
Loss: i.e. loss of Sales Revenue		– (200 000)
Decrease in Overall Profits		(20 000)

■ MAKE OR BUY DECISIONS

A company is producing Component 'X' and set out below are the costs of production.

Component 'X'
Standard Cost per Unit

	£
Direct Materials	6.00
Direct Labour	5.00
Variable Overhead	2.00
Proportion of Factory Overhead	3.00
Total Cost	16.00

The company has been approached by another manufacturer who is ready to supply an identical component at £14.00 per unit. It is estimated that the purchase of the component would entail an additional cost of handling and storing of £0.50 per unit.

SOLUTION

In terms of marginal costing the correct approach is this. Presumably whether or not the company manufactures the component its total fixed costs will remain the same. For the purposes of this particular decision, therefore, we should compare the marginal cost of the component with the cost of purchasing it. Therefore:

Component 'X'
Marginal Cost per Unit

	£
Direct Materials	6.00
Direct Labour	5.00
Variable Overhead	2.00
Total	13.00

As the purchase of the component would result in a total cost per unit of £14.50, it is clearly preferable to make it internally rather than buy outside.

■ ALTERNATIVE METHODS OF OPERATION

A machine is intended to operate throughout a 40-hour week but on average 10 hours of production per week are lost through breakdowns which cost £100 per week to repair.

It has been suggested that a programme of routine preventive maintenance would reduce stoppages, but may increase costs.

Three alternatives are under consideration:

1   To carry out maintenance on Saturdays at a cost of £250 which, it is estimated, would halve the breakdown time and repair costs.

40 hrs. → operation
10 hrs. → production
£100 → reparation

2 To carry out maintenance on a night shift at a weekly cost of £750 which it is estimated would save 90% of the breakdown time and repair costs.
3 To carry on as at present.

Production details are:
Output three tons per hour, saleable at £50 per ton.
Raw materials costs £15 per ton.
Process wages, which are fixed, of £1750 per week.
Required:
A comparative cost statement for the three alternatives.

(Association of Business Executives)

SOLUTION
The critical determinant of profitability here is the contribution achieved per productive hour. This is calculated as follows:

	Per Ton	Per Hour
	£	£
Selling Price	50	150
less Variable Cost	15	45
Contribution	35	105

Now that we have the contribution per hour, we may relate it to the number of hours relevant to each of the three possible methods of operation as shown below.

	(a)	(b)	(c)
Weekly Production Hours	35	39	30
	£	£	£
Contribution per Hour	105	105	105
Potential Weekly Contribution	3 675	4 095	3 150
less Fixed Costs:			
Process Wages	1 750	1 750	1 750
Repairs	50	10	100
Maintenance	250	750	—
Total Fixed Costs	2 050	2 510	1 850
Profit	1 625	1 585	1 300

■ PRICE LEVEL DECISIONS

Jack and Jill are the proprietors of a hairdressing establishment, and set out below is a statement showing typical weekly results.

	Mon	Tue	Wed	Thu	Fri	Sat	Total
Number of customers	20	40	40	60	60	80	300
	£	£	£	£	£	£	£
Sales Revenue	200	400	400	600	600	800	3 000
Fixed Costs	400	400	400	400	400	400	2 400
Variable Costs	20	40	40	60	60	80	300
Total Cost	420	440	440	460	460	480	2 700
Net Profit (Net Loss)	(220)	(40)	(40)	140	140	320	300

The proprietors are not satisfied with the profitability of the establishment and, at a meeting with their business advisers, the following suggestions are made:

1   All charges should be increased by 10 per cent, even though this is likely to lead to a 5 per cent loss of customers.

2   Increase all charges on Thursday, Friday and Saturday only by 20 per cent – this is likely to result in a 10 per cent loss of customers during those three days only.

3   In view of the net loss on Monday, the establishment should open from Tuesday to Saturday and remain closed on Monday.

SOLUTION

		£
1	Present Weekly Sales Revenue	3 000
	less Variable Cost	300
	Present Weekly Contribution	2 700

	£
Suggested change:	
Weekly Sales Revenue (285 × £11)	3 135
less Variable Cost	285
New Weekly Contribution	2 850

Therefore total weekly contribution would increase by £150, thus increasing the weekly net profit from £300 to £450.

		£
2	Present Sales Revenue	
	(Thursday, Friday and Saturday)	2 000
	less Variable Cost	200
	Contribution	1 800

	£
Suggested change:	
Sales Revenue (Thu, Fri, Sat.)	
180 × £12	2 160
less Variable Cost	180
New Contribution (Thu, Fri, Sat.)	1 980

Therefore total weekly contribution would increase by £180, thus increasing the weekly net profit from £300 to £480.

3   The effect of closing the establishment on Monday would be to lose the contribution earned during that day, i.e. (£200 − £20) £180. This would, in turn, decrease the weekly net profit to (£300 − £180) £120.

We would therefore rank the three suggestions as follows:

(b) giving a weekly net profit of £480
(a) giving a weekly net profit of £450
(c) giving a weekly net profit of £120

■ PROFIT PLANNING

Your company manufactures three products, the Alpha, the Beta and the Gamma.

The following information has been given to you from the sales forecast for the month of August 1984:

	Alpha	Beta	Gamma
Forecast demand	50	150	200
Raw materials per unit	£100	£150	£80
Direct labour hours (at £3.00 per hour)	5	8	2

Variable overhead − 10% of total cost of materials and labour.

Fixed overhead is to be apportioned to the products at 150% of total direct labour cost.

Selling price is calculated by adding 50% of total cost.

(a) Calculate
   (i)   the unit selling prices;
   (ii) the contribution per direct labour hour.

(b) Prepare a forecast of the profit for the month of August in sufficient detail to measure the performance of each product.

(c) If the direct labour available in August falls below that required to produce the forecast level, how would you allocate it in order to maximize your profit, assuming that each product may be sold independently and that the labour force can be transferred from one product to another?

Work to the nearest £.   (Institute of Marketing)

SOLUTION

(a) (i)   Unit Selling Prices

	Alpha £	Beta £	Gamma £
Variable Costs:			
Direct Materials	100	150	80
Direct Labour	15	24	6
	115	174	86
add Variable Overhead – 10%	12	17	9
Total Variable Cost	127	191	95
Fixed Overhead (150% of Direct Labour)	23	36	9
Total Cost	150	227	104
add Mark-up (50% of Total Cost)	75	114	52
Unit Selling Price	225	341	156

(a) (ii)   Contribution per Direct Labour Hour

	Alpha £	Beta £	Gamma £
Unit Selling Price	225	341	156
less Variable Cost	127	191	95
Contribution	98	150	61
Direct Labour Hours	5	8	2
Contribution per Direct Labour Hour	£20	£19	£31

(b) Profit Forecast for August 1984

	Alpha £	Beta £	Gamma £	Total £
Unit Selling Price	225	341	156	—
Units to be Sold	50	150	200	—
Sales Revenue	11 250	51 150	31 200	93 600
less Variable Costs:				
Direct Materials	5 000	22 500	16 000	
Direct Labour	750	3 600	1 200	
Variable Overhead	575	2 610	1 720	
	6 325	28 710	18 920	53 955
Contribution	4 925	22 440	12 280	39 645
less Fixed Overhead				8 325
Forecast Net Profit				£31 320

(c) The possible shortage of labour during August means that the availability of labour must be regarded as a critical determinant of profitability, or limiting factor. If, in fact, the supply of labour proves inadequate, it will make sense to use labour in operations where it produces the highest contribution. From our calculations in (a) (ii) it is clear that the company should concentrate on producing Gamma, where the contribution per direct labour hour is £31.

■ SELF ASSESSMENT QUESTIONS

1 A large company's advertising manager has requested board approval to increase this year's advertising budget by £50 000. The advertising manager believes that this extra outlay will increase sales during the year by £300 000. As marketing director, and a member of the board, what other information would you require in order to assess the request?

(Institute of Marketing)

2 Explain the usefulness of the following cost concepts in marginal costing:
(a) sunk cost;
(b) relevant cost;
(c) variable cost.

3 Explain the usefulness of contribution in short-term decision making.

4 Podmore Products is proposing to launch a new product to which the following data applies:

Estimated annual sales volume: 100 000 units @ £25.00
Estimated annual fixed costs:

Marketing	£200 000
Administration	£ 50 000
Production	£250 000

Estimated variable costs:

Selling, etc.	£2.00 per unit
Manufacturing	£8.00 per unit

Estimated average investment in the product: £3 600 000
Target return: 25% ROI.

Assume that the product has been launched and, eight months following the launch, it seems likely that annual sales will be 80 000 units for the next few years. However, a major mail-order firm has offered to buy 20 000 units per annum over the next 3 years at £15.00 per unit.

Required: As the sales manager of Podmore Products, would you accept this order? Justify your decision.

(Institute of Marketing)

5 The Jolly Jelly Company employs four sales people, each covering a large territory. A basic salary of £800 per month is paid, plus a commission at the rate of

1% of sales revenue. All the sales people have expense accounts to cover travelling and entertaining.

Additional data relating to May 1987 is given below:

Sales Team

	Graham	Wendy	Tony	Tina
Days on the road	22	22	22	22
Miles travelled	2 200	3 000	2 800	4 000
Calls made	88	110	66	72
Sales revenue	£200 000	£160 000	£180 000	£240 000
Travelling expenses	£330	£440	£390	£510
Entertaining expenses	£200	£300	£400	£600

Required:
Assume the role of the company's sales manager. Write a report to the marketing director evaluating the performance of each salesperson for the month of May 1987.

(Institute of Marketing)

6 The London Restaurant Company operates, amongst others, the Tower Restaurant. The accountant of the company has prepared the following statement of typical weekly results.

	Mon	Tue	Wed	Thu	Fri	Sat	Total
No. of customers	40	80	100	120	160	200	700
	£	£	£	£	£	£	£
Sales Revenue	400	800	1 000	1 200	1 600	2 000	7 000
Fixed Cost	600	600	600	600	600	600	3 600
Variable Cost	160	320	400	480	640	800	2 800
Total Cost	760	920	1 000	1 080	1 240	1 400	6 400
Net Profit (Net Loss)	(360)	(120)	—	120	360	600	600

Note: (a) Sales revenue per customer amounts to £10.
      (b) Variable costs are incurred at the rate of 40 per cent of sales revenue.

The directors of the company are anxious to improve the profitability of the restaurant. The following suggestions are made.
(a) In view of the losses incurred at the beginning of the week the restaurant should be closed each Monday and Tuesday.
(b) All prices should be increased by 10 per cent, even though this will result in a 5 per cent loss of customers.
(c) All prices should be decreased by 10 per cent as this will certainly increase the number of customers by 15 per cent.
You are required to consider these proposals and state, with reasons, which of the three proposals should be preferred.

(Schiller International University)

7 A manufacturer has been offered an order to make equipment for a new factory. The value of the order is £50 000 which gives a higher profit margin than usual. However, delivery is very urgent and is required in a shorter period than the manufacturer would normally offer. A penalty of £6 000 would be payable for late delivery.

The following estimated costs have been calculated:

	£
Material	10 000
Labour (2500 hours)	15 000
Variable Overhead	5 000
Apportioned Fixed Overhead	10 000
	40 000

If the order is accepted, 2 000 hours of short-term sub-contract work, carried out for another factory, will not be undertaken. This work gives a contribution of £7.50 per hour.

Required:
(a) A statement showing the effect on the profits of the company if the order is accepted.
(b) An indication of the other factors that should be considered before a final decision is reached.

(Association of Business Executives)

8 Let us assume the following are the costs of running your car for 15 000 miles a year:

Petrol 750 gallons @ £2.00	£1 500
Oil changes 6 @ £10	60
Tyre wear (based on life of 20 000 miles; a new set of 4 costs £160)	120
Regular maintenance and repair	330
Insurance	250
Washing and waxing	50
Tax	75
Garage rent & parking charges	300
Depreciation (£10 000 ÷ 4 year life)	2 500
	£5 185

(a) If you drove 10 000 miles per year, what would be the average unit cost per mile? And if you drove 20 000 miles per year?
(b) If you went on a 200 mile journey with a friend who agrees to share the cost of the trip, how much should the friend pay?
(c) Your spouse wants a similar car for shopping and other errands that you now carry out. If you buy a second car it will be driven 3 000 miles per year, but the total mileage for both cars will still be 15 000 per year. What will be the annual cost of operating the second car?

What will be its average unit cost per mile?

(Institute of Marketing)

5 Absorption costing

■ THE ELEMENTS OF COST

Whilst in marginal costing we are concerned with the behaviour of costs, absorption costing looks at the types and nature of costs. The commonly accepted cost classification used in absorption costing is based on what are described as the *elements of cost*. When we analyse the total cost of a product we may distinguish the following elements.

> Direct Materials
> \+ Direct Labour
> \+ Direct Expenses   = Prime Cost
> > *add*
> Production Overheads   = Production Cost
> > *add*
> Selling Overheads
> \+ Distribution Overheads
> \+ Administration Overheads = Total Cost

Prime cost

This consists of three elements, as follows.

DIRECT MATERIALS
This includes all expenditure on materials which may be traced to the units of output (sometimes described as 'cost units'). The cost of flour in bread; the cost of meat in a steak and the cost of timber in a chair – are all direct costs because they become part of the product.

DIRECT LABOUR
This includes the cost of labour which is directly associated with the manufacture of the products concerned. To revert to our previous examples, the

wages paid to the bakers, cooks and cabinet makers would be regarded as direct wages.

DIRECT EXPENSES
These include expenditure which, although directly relevant to the manufacture of a product, cannot be traced to the units of output. Examples of such expenditure would be special moulds, designs or drawings specifically required for given products.

Production overheads

Production overheads include three elements, as follows.

INDIRECT MATERIALS
For instance, materials used in the course of manufacture which do not become part of the product. Examples of indirect materials are: soaps, floor polish, detergents, lubricants, dustbins, books for the technical library, etc.

INDIRECT LABOUR
This consists of the cost of factory/works labour which is not directly or immediately involved in the manufacture of particular units of output. Typical examples of indirect labour are the wages and salaries paid to: supervisors, inspectors, factory cleaners, timekeepers, storekeepers, etc.

INDIRECT EXPENSES
These consist of a fairly large number of items of expenditure such as rent and rates, heat, light and power, depreciation, insurance, canteen, welfare, etc.

Selling overheads

These consist of expenditure involved in securing orders for the products of the company. The principal items of expenditure are as follows:
 (a) Salaries and commissions paid to sales managers, sales representatives, merchandisers and sales staff.
 (b) Press and television advertising.
 (c) Selling expenses – including depreciation of vehicles and motoring expenses.
 (d) The cost of brochures, catalogues, price lists and other promotional material.

Distribution overheads

These consist of, basically, the cost of warehousing and delivery of the goods to the customers. The main items of expenditure here are:
 (a) Warehousing wages and salaries.

(b) Warehouse rent, rates and electricity.
(c) Repairs to and depreciation of vehicles.
(d) Cost of packing cases, wrapping paper/materials, etc.

Administration overheads

These include a large number of expenses incurred in the management and administration of an enterprise. The principal items of expenditure here are:
(a) Salaries and wages of managers, clerks, etc.
(b) Rent and rates.
(c) Office supplies – including printing and stationery.
(d) Lighting and heating.
(e) Repairs to and depreciation of office furniture, machinery and equipment.
(f) Financial charges – including legal fees, bank charges and audit fees.

■ ABSORPTION COSTING: PROCEDURE

The most important feature of absorption costing is the transfer of the costs associated with production to individual units of output. This procedure consists of three stages as described below.

Allocation and apportionment

The first stage is to charge all the costs to the cost centres set up for this purpose. A cost centre may be a department or section of a business; it may consist of several employees or even one person. Cost centres are typically set up within the principal functions, i.e. production, selling, distribution and administration.

Whilst it is possible to regard a whole function as a cost centre, it is usual to divide each function into a number of cost centres. Thus where production consists of three processes, e.g. turning, assembling and painting, each of these three would normally constitute a separate cost centre.

There are two ways in which costs are charged to cost centres.

(a) Some costs are *allocated* to cost centres. Allocation takes place when a whole cost is charged to the cost centre in which it has originated. The wages paid to the painters in the above example would be allocated to that cost centre. Allocation is simple as we know where, so to speak, the expenditure belongs and, simply, place it where it has arisen.

(b) Other costs are *apportioned*. Apportionment takes place where a cost has to be split on some fair basis between two or more cost centres. To revert to our last example, if there is a production manager responsible for the three cost centres (turning, assembling and painting) his or her salary will be apportioned and charged – so much to each of the three cost centres.

Different bases of apportionment will be used in relation to different costs. Some of the typical examples are given below.

(a) Rent, rates, lighting and heating as well as depreciation of premises may be apportioned on the basis of space occupied.

(b) Depreciation, insurance and the cost of maintenance may be apportioned on the basis of the book value of the assets concerned.

(c) The cost of the works canteen, supervision, safety and medical services provided will normally be apportioned on the basis of the number of employees in each cost centre.

Cost centres are of two kinds. Some are described as *production cost centres*, and these are the cost centres where the actual production and manufacturing process takes place. Others are described as *service cost centres*, and these are cost centres which assist the production cost centres. Examples of service cost centres are purchasing, stores, works canteen, etc. Where there are three production cost centres, A, B, and C and two service cost centres X and Y, this first stage of allocating and apportioning costs to cost centres would be as illustrated in Fig. 11.

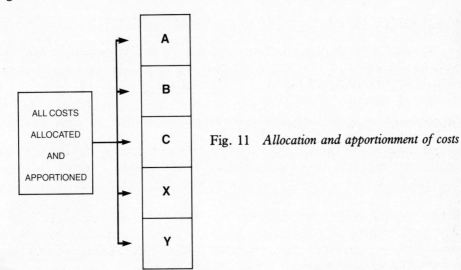

Fig. 11 *Allocation and apportionment of costs*

Transferring costs to production cost centres

Once the first stage (of allocation and apportionment) has been completed, it is necessary to transfer all the costs of the service cost centres to the production cost centres. This is illustrated in Fig. 12.

Students will appreciate that, after the completion of this second stage, all the costs are within the production cost centres.

Absorption of service centre costs

The third and final stage in the long procedure of absorption costing is the allotment of costs from the cost centres to the units of output produced (i.e. cost

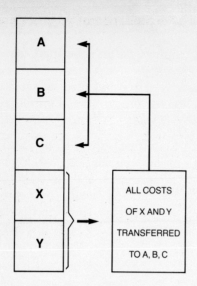

Fig. 12 *Transfer of service cost centre costs to production cost centres*

units). The basic aim of this process of absorption is twofold, i.e. to ensure that (a) each unit of output carries – in addition to its prime cost – the right proportion of service centre costs, and (b) all the costs transferred to the production cost centres are absorbed by the individual units of output.

Let us assume that our three production cost centres manufacture altogether six products: a, b, c, d, e and f. The process of absorption will have to ensure that all the costs within A, B and C are transferred to and absorbed by the six products. This is illustrated in Fig. 13.

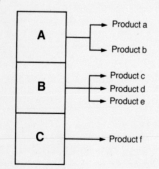

Fig. 13 *Absorption of overheads by individual products*

One final point needs to be made with regard to the process of absorption costing. Most of the costs incurred under the headings of selling overheads, distribution overheads and administration overheads, are fixed costs and, frequently, costs which are difficult to associate with the manufacture of individual products. Quite often, therefore, the only costs which are transferred to production cost centres and subsequently absorbed by units of output are production overheads. All other overheads – selling, distribution and administration overheads – are still subject to strict periodic controls, but are not subject to the process of absorption costing.

■ METHODS OF ABSORPTION

In many manufacturing situations there are a number of different products being manufactured; and these may vary considerably in terms of cost absorption. Some may be time consuming and be labour intensive; others may require little labour but be heavily dependent on specialized plant and machinery.

Different units of output will, therefore, require the application of different methods of absorption. Students should remember, however, that most overheads are incurred with the passage of time, and methods of absorption should therefore recognize the time element as important in this context. Let us now look at the main methods of absorption.

Percentage on direct wages

This method is simple and easy to apply and therefore widely used. Its advantage is that it takes into consideration the element of time. It does not, however, take into account the fact that there may be different types of labour with, consequently, different rates of pay. Also the method does not distinguish between manual production and machine production.

The percentage on direct wages method may be illustrated as shown below.

JOB NO : 001

	£
Direct Materials	400.00
Direct Labour	160.00
Direct Expenses	40.00
Prime Cost	600.00
add Production Overheads – 50% of Direct Labour	80.00
Production Cost	680.00

Percentage on direct materials

This method is sound only in situations where production overheads are significantly related to the cost of materials; and this is quite uncommon. The method does not take into account the time element. Although it is quite often used – mainly in small businesses and because of its simplicity – it is not really suitable for most types of manufacturing situations. The application of the method is illustrated below.

JOB NO : 002

	£
Direct Materials	600.00
Direct Labour	400.00
Direct Expenses	50.00
Prime Cost	1 050.00
add Production Overhead – 20% of Direct Materials	120.00
Production Cost	1 170.00

Percentage on prime cost

This method has – as the previous two – the advantage of simplicity; and this presumably explains its popularity and wide use in industry. Where, however, the component of materials cost is much greater than that of labour, it will not give sufficient recognition to the element of time. An example follows.

JOB NO: 003

	£
Direct Materials	200.00
Direct Labour	400.00
Direct Expenses	50.00
Prime Cost	650.00
add Production Overhead – 50% of Prime Cost	325.00
Production Cost	975.00

Hourly rates of recovery

The three methods of absorption, although in common use in many industries, do not always give satisfactory results. For greater precision it is preferable to use either: (a) a machine hour rate or (b) a direct labour hour rate. This is particularly so in situations where there are several different processes taking place or where there are several different jobs/products involved.

Students will remember that the basic aim of the process is to ensure that all production overheads are absorbed in the cost units (units of output). The method is illustrated below.

	Dept X	*Dept* Y
	£	£
Production Overheads	80 000	70 000
Machine Hours	20 000	4 000
Direct Labour Hours	6 000	25 000
Direct Labour Cost	14 500	63 230

The machine hour rates will be:

$$\frac{£80\ 000}{20\ 000} = £4.00 \text{ per hour in Dept X}$$

$$\frac{£70\ 000}{4\ 000} = £17.50 \text{ per hour in Dept Y}$$

The direct labour hour rates will be:

$$\frac{£80\ 000}{6\ 000} = £13.33 \text{ per direct labour hour in Dept X}$$

$$\frac{£70\ 000}{25\ 000} = £2.80 \text{ per direct labour hour in Dept Y}$$

■ ABSORPTION COSTING V. MARGINAL COSTING

Now that we have described the process of absorption costing let us compare it with marginal costing. There are four main differences between the two techniques, and these may be summarized as follows.

(a) In marginal costing we are concerned with the *behaviour of costs* and use cost concepts such as 'fixed cost', 'variable cost' and 'semi-fixed cost'. The criterion for cost classification in absorption costing is different. Here we look at the *type of cost* and use cost concepts such as 'direct materials', 'direct labour', 'direct expense', 'production overhead', etc.

(b) In marginal costing we emphasize the *element of contribution*, and calculate contribution for each product, process, department, etc. Fixed costs are, so to speak, kept in the background. In absorption costing the stress is on the *full cost concept*: we arrive at the cost of each product by adding to its prime cost a proportion of factory/production overheads and, sometimes, a proportion of selling, distribution and administration overheads. The stress, therefore, is on the total cost per unit of output.

(c) Marginal costing is essentially a technique designed to help with *short-run decisions*. Absorption costing does not distinguish between fixed and variable costs, and hence *does not provide the relevant information for short-run decisions*. It is, therefore, more suitable for steady, normal – indeed uneventful – conditions where the need for frequent decisions on matters such as size of output, selling prices, etc. does not arise.

(d) Proponents of absorption costing claim that its advantage is that, as each unit of output has been charged with an element of indirect costs, there is *less danger of under-recovery of overheads*. With marginal costing there may be a tendency for the selling prices to be set at too low a level, which may well produce some contribution but, nevertheless, fail to secure satisfactory overall profitability.

■ SELF ASSESSMENT QUESTIONS

1 Explain the method of absorption costing.
2 Compare and contrast Marginal Costing and Absorption Costing.

(Association of Business Executives)

3 Pressure Pumps Ltd manufacture two pumps, A and B, to which the following data relates:

	Product A	Product B
Direct Materials	£38.60	£51.40
Direct Labour		
Machining at £4.50 per hour	6 hours	6 hours
Assembly at £3.60 per hour	2 hours	4 hours
Budgeted quantity of production for 1988	40 000 pumps	20 000 pumps

Overhead for the year is estimated at £1 286 000.

Required:
(a) Calculate the following absorption rates:
   (i)   Materials Cost percentage rate
   (ii) Prime Cost percentage rate
   (iii) Direct Labour hour rate
   (iv) Machine hour rate
(b) State, with reasons, which overhead absorption rates you consider most appropriate in this case.
(c) State the main arguments for the use of budgeted overhead rates rather than historical rates of overhead absorption.

(Association of Business Executives)

4 You work as the Accountant for an expanding company making aluminium components. Production is clearly segregated into three separate departments: moulding, fabrication and finishing.

You should note that the nature of each department varies greatly:

Moulding uses expensive machines, few workers and common types of materials.

Fabrication employs large numbers of skilled workers of differing grades and few expensive machines.

Finishing mainly involves some hand finishing and hand paint spraying.

You are required to:

(a) Describe the purpose of overhead absorption rates.

(b) State which overhead absorption method is best suited to each department justifying your choice.

(Association of Business Executives – Modified)

6 | Budgetary control

■ INTRODUCTION

Budgetary control is a technique in common use in all medium-sized and large organizations. Also it is a technique which is frequently the subject of examination questions. Students are, therefore, well advised to study the present chapter carefully.

A *budget* is a financial and quantitative statement – drawn up and approved prior to the budget year – which shows the policy to be pursued to achieve a given objective. Several points are worth noting in relation to this definition.

1   A budget is not the same as a forecast. Whilst forecast figures show likely trends and happenings in the future, budgeted figures reflect the policy and intention of management with regard to what should or ought to take place. The discussion of budgeted and forecast costs in Chapter 2 is relevant in this context.

2   Budgets are, typically, prepared for one year. Where the budget year commences on 1 January, the actual process of preparing the budget will commence in September/October so that it may be submitted for approval before the end of the current year.

3   All budgets are expressed in terms of money but, frequently, it is desirable to show the relevant quantities. Thus the sales budget will usually show the number of units; the labour cost budget may well show the budgeted time for the completion of certain tasks/operations, etc.

4   A budget cannot be prepared except on the basis of a clear perception of what the organization wants to achieve. This, in practice, means that we have to have clearly stated decisions on the specific aims for the budget year concerned. Such decisions will encompass the profit target, sales revenue, share of the market, etc. A budget is, therefore, a practical expression of the aims of the organization as well as management policy.

Budgetary control is concerned with executive responsibility. It assigns responsibility for various parts of the overall budget to individual executives. Periodically, we compare actual with budgeted results to establish to what extent the targets set to such executives have been achieved. From this it follows that budgets are important tools for the evaluation of executive performance.

It is important to ensure that, in terms of authority and responsibility, budgets are prepared sensibly and realistically. Where an executive has no control over some expenditure, he or she should not be held responsible for it. For example, the marketing director has normally no control over the cost of rent, rates, etc. and, therefore, there seems to be little point in showing such expenditure in the marketing budget. Where, for some reason, such uncontrollable items of expenditure are shown, it should be clearly understood that, as they are uncontrollable, no responsibility for adverse variances should attach to the executive concerned.

■ ORGANIZATIONAL ASPECTS

BUDGET COMMITTEE

Where there is a system of budgetary control there is normally constituted a budget committee. This consists of the principal senior executives of the business with, often, the chief executive or his/her deputy acting as chairman and the management accountant as secretary.

The budget committee has two main tasks: (a) to ensure that there is sufficient co-ordination in the preparation of budgets and (b) to ensure the smooth operation of the system of budgetary control.

Budget review period

Budgeting is an annual exercise, but it is essential to review the progress of the business more frequently than once a year. It is important, therefore, to divide the budget year into convenient shorter periods for review purposes. There are a number of possible solutions here and actual practice differs from one company and industry to another. What is important is that review periods should be such as to facilitate the preparation and presentation of: weekly, monthly, quarterly, half-yearly and annual reports – as some reports will be prepared more frequently than others. Some common solutions are: (a) to divide the budget year into 12 calendar months; (b) to divide it into 13 lunar months (of four weeks); (c) to divide the year into four quarters, each of which consists of three 'months' of five, four and four weeks. The three possibilities are illustrated in Fig. 14.

BUDGET MANUAL

It is essential to maintain a budget manual. This will describe in detail all the budgetary procedures such as:
- what budgets are to be prepared;
- dates for submission of budget reports;
- to whom each report is to be presented, etc.

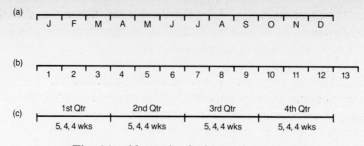

Fig. 14 *Alternative budget review periods*

Also the budget manual should contain a classification and coding of accounts to ensure that all income and expenditure are recorded consistently from one period to another. The cost of printing promotional material is a marketing expense and should not be regarded as 'printing and stationery' one year, and 'advertising' the following year. Such possible anomalies can only be prevented by a sufficiently detailed classification of all items of income and expenditure.

Preparation of the budget

The preparation of the budget usually consists of five essential stages as described below.

1 INITIAL FORECASTS
The first and most important stage is to look at the external environment and make some preliminary forecasts and assessments. It is important to consider the likely developments in the national economy and probable changes in the market place as well as changes in technology, etc.

2 DEVELOPMENT OF POLICY
Next, we attempt to develop the policy of the business which obviously has to take account of the external environment. Decisions which are relevant at this stage relate to the range of products to be produced (or services offered), size of output, channels of distribution, etc.

3 OPERATIONS PLANNING
Having decided what to produce, we consider in some detail the operational requirements such as: quantities of raw materials, size of labour force as well as the necessary plant and equipment. It is this process of operations planning that results in the formulation of the initial budget.

4 FORMALIZATION OF BUDGETS
Once the initial budgets have been prepared, it is necessary to examine them in detail to ensure that all the planning undertaken in 3 above results in a well co-ordinated plan which: (a) guarantees a streamlined, smooth operation, and

(b) reflects the intentions and policy of management in terms of the aims chosen for the budget year.

5 APPROVAL

The final step is the approval of the budgets by the board of directors. The budgets then become formal documents, reflecting the policy of the company and assigning specific responsibilities to the executives concerned.

Kinds of budgets

The various budgets prepared by an organization may be classified in several different ways.

From the point of view of the subject-matter of the budget, we may distinguish:

1 Capital budgets which deal with the assets and liabilities of the organization. Examples of capital budgets are: plant and equipment budget, debtors and creditors budgets, cash budget.
2 Operating budgets, which deal with current income and expenditure. Examples of operating budgets are: sales budget, cost of sales budget, labour cost budget, marketing budget, etc.

From the point of view of the comprehensiveness of the budgets, we may distinguish:

1 Functional budgets, which relate to the principal functions or organizational structure of the business. Examples of functional budgets are: marketing budget, production budget, administration budget, research and development budget.
2 Master budgets, which consolidate the various operating or functional budgets. There are essentially two master budgets: the budgeted profit and loss account and the budgeted balance sheet.

From the point of view of the impact of the level of activity assumed in the budget, we may distinguish:

1 Fixed budgets, which are not affected by changes in the level of activity (i.e. production or sales revenue). Examples of fixed budgets are budgets for fixed overheads, financial charges (e.g. interest on capital, repayment of borrowed funds) and management salaries.
2 Flexible budgets, which are dependent on the budgeted sales volume. Thus budgets for the cost of sales, direct labour, direct expense, salesmen's commissions, etc. will be flexible budgets.

Now that we have dealt with the procedural and theoretical aspects of budgetary control let us look at some practical examples.

Cash budgets

The basic procedure for the preparation of the cash budget is as follows. We start with the opening cash balance, add the budgeted cash inflows, deduct the budgeted cash outflows and the result is the budgeted cash balance at the end of the period. Particulars of the budgeted cash inflows and cash outflows will be obtained from various budgets. Thus the budgeted cash outflows in respect of raw materials will be extracted from the production budget or the cost of sales budget; the budgeted cash outflow in respect of direct wages will be obtained from the labour cost budget; the budgeted cash inflow in respect of cash and credit sales will be obtained from the sales budget or the marketing budget.

EXAMPLE

Walter Wall Carpets Ltd has found itself with an <u>unexpected cash flow</u> problem and the company's bank has asked for a cash budget to be prepared for the first six months of 1987.

The following information is available:

	Sales: 1986 (Actual) 1987 (Forecast)	(£000s) Labour and Raw Material Costs
1986		
November	90 000	60 000
December	90 000	10 000
1987		
January	30 000	30 000
February	30 000	30 000
March	60 000	90 000
April	180 000	110 000
May	220 000	120 000
June	240 000	140 000

Collection periods for sales are:

- Cash sales are 10% of sales each month.
- 60% is collected in the month following the month of sale. The remainder is collected in the second month following sale. Bad debts are negligible.
- Payments for labour and raw materials are made the month following the one in which they are incurred.
- General and administrative expenses are £15 000 per month paid the month in which they are incurred. Depreciation charges are £12 000 per month. Tax payments are due in January of £60 000 and April of £20 000. The opening cash balance is £20 000 overdrawn. Ignore interest on overdraft.

Required:

A monthly cash budget for the first six months of 1987.

(Association of Business Executives)

SOLUTION

When preparing the cash budget it is important to take into account the time lags both in respect of the cash inflow and cash outflow. The cash inflow for January is:

(a) £3 000 – which is 10 per cent of January sales;
(b) £54 000 – which is 60 per cent of December sales;
(c) £27 000 – which is 30 per cent of November sales.

Cash Budget
for six months ending 30 June 1987

	Jan £	Feb £	Mar £	Apr £	May £	June £
Opening Balance	(20 000)	(21 000)	(18 000)	(30 000)	(72 000)	(49 000)
Cash Inflow:						
Cash Sales (10%)	3 000	3 000	6 000	18 000	22 000	24 000
First Month (60%)	54 000	18 000	18 000	36 000	108 000	132 000
Second Month (30%)	27 000	27 000	9 000	9 000	18 000	54 000
Total	64 000	27 000	15 000	33 000	76 000	161 000
Cash Outflow:						
Labour and Raw Materials	10 000	30 000	30 000	90 000	110 000	120 000
Gen and Admin Expenses	15 000	15 000	15 000	15 000	15 000	15 000
Tax Payments	60 000					20 000
Total	85 000	45 000	45 000	105 000	125 000	155 000
Closing Balance	(21 000)	(18 000)	(30 000)	(72 000)	(49 000)	6 000

N.B. Students will note that the depreciation charges of £12 000 per month mentioned in the question do not appear in the cash budget. Depreciation is a non-cash expense – i.e. it does not entail a cash outflow and must not therefore be shown in the cash budget.

Sales budget

This is a budget which is normally difficult to prepare. In order to ensure that it is realistic and sufficiently accurate, it is necessary to consider a number of external factors such as: general business conditions; the state of the national economy; government fiscal and other policies; the products offered by competitors, etc. Also it is essential to take into account several internal factors which may influence the sales budget, e.g. plant capacity, any new marketing and sales promotion strategies, availability of skilled labour, and finally the basic aims of the organization set for the forthcoming budget year.

EXAMPLE

The ABC Co. Ltd sells three products, A, B and C in two territories, North and South.

The budgeted sales for 19.. are as follows:

North:	A – 130 000 units	South:	A – 104 000 units
	B – 325 000 units		B – 286 000 units
	C – 156 000 units		C – 91 000 units

Assume that the annual sales budget is divided into 13 lunar months and show a sales budget report for Month 1 when actual sales were:

North:	A – 11 000 units	South:	A – 8 800 units
	B – 24 000 units		B – 21 000 units
	C – 13 000 units		C – 7 400 units

Budgeted and actual selling prices were:

North	Budget	Actual	South	Budget	Actual
A	£10.00	£10.50	A	£10.00	£10.20
B	6.00	5.80	B	6.00	5.90
C	12.00	11.00	C	12.00	11.50

The layout of a monthly sales budget report may take several different forms, depending on individual preferences and the degree of detail one wishes to show. The report which follows is, however, fairly typical.

Sales budget report
Month 1

		Budget			Actual			Variance	
	Qty	Price	Value	Qty	Price	Value	Fav	Adv
	—	£	£	—	£	£	£	£
North: A	10 000	10.00	100 000	11 000	10.50	115 500	15 500	
B	25 000	6.00	150 000	24 000	5.80	139 200		10 800
C	12 000	12.00	144 000	13 000	11.00	143 000		1 000
South: A	8 000	10.00	80 000	8 800	10.20	89 760	9 760	
B	22 000	6.00	132 000	21 000	5.90	123 900		8 100
C	7 000	12.00	84 000	7 400	11.50	85 100	1 100	
Total	84 000	—	690 000	85 200	—	696 460	26 360	19 900

It is important, in a report of this kind, to show the variances – favourable or adverse – in order to provide a meaningful comparison between what was planned and what was achieved.

Selling and distribution cost budget

The budget for selling and distribution expenses may, in fact, consist of two separate budgets – one for selling expenses and one for distribution expenses.

The main selling expenses will include: sales staff salaries, sales commissions, travelling and motoring expenses. Also included under this heading would be:

rent and rates, office expenses, postage, telephone and, of course, the cost of advertising and public relations.

The main distribution expenses will relate to warehousing, packing and the transportation of the goods. Typical examples here will be: rent and rates of warehouses and depots; wages of warehousemen, packers, drivers; salaries paid to managers, foremen, supervisors and clerks; depreciation of premises, vehicles and equipment, etc. A pro forma selling and distribution cost budget is shown below.

Selling and distribution cost budget

Particulars	North	South	Total
	£	£	£
Sales office:			
Rent and rates	XXX	XXX	XXX
Salaries	XXX	XXX	XXX
Office expenses	XXX	XXX	XXX
Depreciation	XXX	XXX	XXX
Other expenses	XXX	XXX	XXX
Advertising:			
Press	XXX	XXX	XXX
Television	XXX	XXX	XXX
Direct mail	XXX	XXX	XXX
Merchandising	XXX	XXX	XXX
Selling expenses:			
Sales staff salaries	XXX	XXX	XXX
Sales staff commission	XXX	XXX	XXX
Sales staff expenses	XXX	XXX	XXX
Car expenses	XXX	XXX	XXX
Distribution expenses:			
Warehouse wages	XXX	XXX	XXX
Rent and rates	XXX	XXX	XXX
Lorry expenses	XXX	XXX	XXX
Depreciation	XXX	XXX	XXX
Insurance	XXX	XXX	XXX
Other expenses	XXX	XXX	XXX
Total	XXX	XXX	XXX

Marketing budget

Quite frequently a company will have a marketing budget comprising the sales budget and the selling and distribution cost budget, rather than separate budgets for sales, selling expenses and distribution expenses. Set out below is a marketing budget presented in summary form.

Marketing Budget
Year ending 31 December 19..

Particulars	North		South		Total	
	£000	%	£000	%	£000	%
Sales revenue:						
Product A	1 300	25.4	1 040	27.0	2 340	26.1
Product B	1 950	38.1	1 716	44.6	3 666	40.9
Product C	1 872	36.5	1 092	28.4	2 964	33.0
Total	5 122	100.0	3 848	100.0	8 970	100.0
Selling and distribution expenses:						
Sales office	205	4.0	187	4.9	392	4.4
Advertising	154	3.0	140	3.6	294	3.3
Selling expenses	230	4.5	188	4.9	418	4.6
Distribution expenses	151	2.9	135	3.5	286	3.2
Total	740	14.4	650	16.9	1 390	15.5

■ BUDGETING: A COMPREHENSIVE EXAMPLE

The London Toy Co. Ltd commenced operations in December 19.. with a capital of £600 000, which was raised through an issue of 600 000 ordinary shares of £1.00 each. The proceeds of the share issue were paid into the company bank account. During the course of December a number of transactions took place and these are summarized below.

Cash Summary December 19..

	£	£
Cash Received – Share Issue		600 000
less Leasehold Premises (20 years)	300 000	
Plant (estimated life: 10 years)	80 000	
Equipment (estimated life: 10 years)	160 000	
Tools	20 000	
Raw materials	10 000	570 000
Cash Balance Available		30 000

You are given the following additional information.

(a) Sales – these are budgeted as follows: £80 000 in Jaunary; £160 000 in February and £240 000 in subsequent months. Fifty per cent of the sales will be cash sales and the other 50 per cent credit sales. The period of credit extended to customers will be one month.

(b) Raw materials – the cost of raw materials will amount to 40 per cent of the sales revenue. Half the materials cost for any one month will be paid in cash; the other half will be purchased on credit and paid for during the month following purchase.

(c) The company intends to keep a stock of raw materials of £10 000 throughout the year.

(d) Direct wages – these will be incurred at the rate of £50 000 per month. No time lag is expected here.

(e) Other expenses – depreciation on premises, plant and equipment will be calculated on the straight-line basis. The tools will be re-valued annually and it is expected that annual losses will amount to 20 per cent. All other expenses will be incurred at the rate of £40 000 per month – the time lag here will be one month.

You are asked to prepare the company's Cash Budget, a budgeted Profit and Loss Account for the first six months of operations and a budgeted Balance Sheet as at 30th June 19...

SOLUTION

Cash Budget for six months ending 30 June 19..

	Jan	Feb	Mar	Apr	May	Jun	Notes
	£000	£000	£000	£000	£000	£000	
Opening Balance	30	4	(14)	16	70	124	
Cash Inflow:							
Cash Sales	40	80	120	120	120	120	Debtors–
Credit Sales		40	80	120	120	120	£120 000
Total	70	124	186	256	310	364	
Cash Outflow:							
Raw Material Cash	16	32	48	48	48	48	Creditors–
Raw Material Credit		16	32	48	48	48	£48 000
Direct Wages	50	50	50	50	50	50	Accr. Exps
Other Expenses		40	40	40	40	40	£40 000
Total	66	138	170	186	186	186	
Closing Balance	4	(14)	16	70	124	178	

Cash Budget: explanatory notes

(a) Students should note that depreciation is not shown in the cash budget which is prepared on a cash basis; depreciation is a non-cash expense.

(b) It is essential to remember the time lags – in our example in respect of credit sales, credit purchases and payments for expenses.

(c) It is useful to have a 'Notes' column – this is helpful in the preparation of the balance sheet.

Budgeted Profit and Loss Account
for six months ending 30 June 19..

	£	£		£
Cost of Sales	480 000		Sales	1 200 000
Direct Wages	300 000	780 000		
Operating Profit		420 000		
		1 200 000		1 200 000
Depreciation:			Operating Profit	420 000
Premises	7 500			
Plant	4 000			
Equipment	8 000			
Tools	2 000	21 500		
Other expenses		240 000		
Net Profit		158 500		
		420 000		420 000

Budgeted Profit and Loss Account: explanatory notes

(a) The budgeted Profit and Loss Account is prepared on a different basis from the Cash Budget. In the latter we are interested in actual flows of cash; in the former we are interested in flows of income and expenditure.

(b) Depreciation is an expense but does not entail a cash outflow: it is, therefore, shown in the budgeted Profit and Loss Account but ignored in the preparation of the Cash Budget.

Budgeted Balance Sheet
as at 30 June 19..

Authorized and Issued Capital	£		*Fixed Assets*			
				Cost	*Dep'n*	*Net*
				£	£	£
600 000 Ord. Shares of £1 each	600 000		Premises	300 000	7 500	292 500
Reserves			Plant	80 000	4 000	76 000
Profit and Loss Account	158 500		Equipt.	160 000	8 000	152 000
			Tools	20 000	2 000	18 000
				560 000	21 500	538 500
Current Liabilities			*Current Assets*			
Creditors	48 000		Raw Materials		10 000	
Accrued Expenses	40 000	88 000	Debtors		120 000	
			Cash		178 000	308 000
		846 500				846 500

Budgeted Balance Sheet: explanatory notes

(a) Particulars of fixed assets would be obtained from the previous balance sheet. Reference would also have to be made to the Capital Expenditure Budget and Budgeted Profit and Loss Account – to ascertain budgeted depreciation.

(b) Budgeted debtors, creditors and cash balance would be obtained from the Cash Budget.

(c) Budgeted net profit would be obtained from the Budgeted Profit and Loss Account.

(d) Particulars of the share capital as well as any debentures, reserves, etc. would be obtained from the previous Balance Sheet.

Flexible budgets

There are many situations in which it is extremely difficult to estimate the future level of activity. This applies particularly to business operations affected by weather conditions (e.g. seaside hotels, sale of ice cream, etc.), economic climate (sale of luxury goods) as well as new ventures where past figures are not available.

In such situations it is usual to prepare a budget for a range of possible levels of output/sales. Once the actual output/sales figures are known, it is possible to prepare a '*flexed budget*', appropriate to that particular level of output/sales. Fixed costs will, of course, not be affected and will not need to be flexed – only the variable cost will require an adjustment.

EXAMPLE

The three possible levels of output for the forthcoming months and the budgeted sales and costs are shown below.

No. of Units	10 000	20 000	30 000
	£	£	£
Sales Revenue	50 000	100 000	150 000
Direct Materials	10 000	20 000	30 000
Labour	24 000	44 000	64 000
Overheads	8 000	8 000	8 000
Total	42 000	72 000	102 000
Profit	8 000	28 000	48 000

Let us assume that the actual number of units was 12 000. A flexible budget may then be prepared as follows:

(a) Direct Materials – these are £1.00 per unit and so for 12 000 units the cost would be £12 000.

(b) Overheads – these are obviously fixed.

(c) Labour – is a semi-fixed cost; and we can split this semi-fixed cost into fully fixed and fully variable elements using the high-low points method explained in Chapter 2.

	Units	£
High Point	20 000	44 000
Low Point	10 000	24 000
Change	10 000	20 000

From the above calculation we see that a change in output of 10 000 units causes a change in the cost of labour of £20 000. The variable cost of labour per unit of output is, therefore, £2. The fixed element may be found as follows.

No. of Units	10 000	20 000
	£	£
Variable Cost @ £2.00 per Unit	20 000	40 000
Which means that the fixed element must be	4 000	4 000
To give budgeted labour costs of	24 000	44 000

The flexed budget for 12 000 units is therefore:

No. of Units	12 000
	£
Sales Revenue	60 000
Direct Materials	12 000
Labour (£24 000 + £4 000)	28 000
Overheads	8 000
Total	48 000
Profit	12 000

Zero-based budgeting

Zero-based budgeting is a relatively new concept which – many accountants claim – is a powerful device of cost control.

With normal budgeting processes the procedure is, quite often, for an executive to ask for whatever he or she was allocated the previous year, plus – say – 10 per cent to take care of inflation and/or enable some new desirable expenditure. Thus a personnel and training manager may have had a budget of £100 000 and would then ask for an additional £15 000 for the following budget year.

This kind of approach has obvious dangers as the budget committee would, in such circumstances, tend to assume that the executive should be allowed the £100 000 in any case, and concentrate their attention on the additional £15 000 being requested. This approach is not always right as there is no guarantee that, in this particular example, the £100 000 is wholly justified. The danger with such annual adjustments of previous-year figures is that, where there is inefficiency and operational mediocrity, it tends to be perpetuated by the system of budgetary control.

The zero-base concept in budgeting is radically different: a manager must justify every £1 requested in his or her budget proposal. With this approach the personnel and training manager would have to explain and justify all the expenditure requested – the whole £115 000.

Zero-based budgeting means more work for managers as, most certainly, it is more time-consuming. However, the zero-base concept results in a thorough review of all proposed expenditure and thus tends to ensure more cost consciousness and operational efficiency.

Advantages of budgetary control

From our discussion of budgetary control students will realize that it has several important advantages and these may be summarized as follows.

(a) The preparation of the budget entails a lot of time spent on the consideration of the principal aims of the organization. All senior executives are, in consequence, more conscious of what has to be achieved.

(b) Budgetary control assigns responsibility to individual executives who, as a result, have a greater realization of their responsibility and are strongly motivated to achieve the targets set for them.

(c) The process of budgeting enables all senior executives to contribute their ideas and participate in the principal decisions involved. This leads to a greater acceptance of budgets by those responsible for their achievement.

(d) Budgeting results in a better co-ordination of the operations – as every functional/departmental budget is discussed and commented upon by all members of the budget committee.

(e) Budgetary control promotes cost consciousness – particularly where the zero-base concept is used – and this results in greater efficiency and enhanced profitability.

(f) Budgeting is the best practical method of giving effect to the intentions/policy of management and thus ensuring the right degree of financial well-being of the organization.

■ SELF ASSESSMENT QUESTIONS

1 Explain what you understand by:
(a) budgetary control;
(b) zero-based budgets;
(c) flexible budgets.
2 Discuss three major advantages of budgetary control.

(Association of Business Executives)

3 Distinguish clearly between:
(a) capital budgets and operating budgets;
(b) functional budgets and master budgets;
(c) fixed budgets and flexible budgets.

4 In late February 1985, Drug Products requested a short-term loan of £16 000 from the bank to finance stocks for a peak of sales predicted for April. The company's plan was to borrow the sum on 1 March and repay on 31 May together with 10% interest.

The following budgeted information is available for the next three months:

	March	April	May
Sales	£30 000	£40 000	£20 000
Purchases of Raw Materials	24 000	12 000	8 000
Wages	4 000	4 500	3 000
Lease Payments	3 000	3 000	3 000
Other Cash Expenses	4 000	6 000	3 000
Depreciation	1 000	1 000	1 000
Net Profit	3 000	6 000	1 000
Fixed Asset Purchases	2 000	—	—

On 1 March the company has a bank balance of £4 000 and debtors on that date are £16 800, of which £15 600 is estimated will be collected during the month and £800 in April. The remainder probably will be uncollectable. The average collection pattern for credit sales is 20% during the month of sale, 75% in the month following sale and 4% in the month following.

Also on 1 March the creditors balances were £18 000, representing February purchases of raw materials, and all purchases are paid for in the month following purchase.

Required:
A Cash Budget for March, April and May 1985 assuming the loan is granted and repaid as planned, showing the resulting bank balance on 1 June.

(Association of Business Executives)

5 *Bamford Sales Office*
The actual expenditure of the Bamford regional sales office of ABC Ltd during the 12 months to 31 May 1986 was:

Salaries

Branch Manager	£12 000	
Salesmen (5 @ £7 500)	£37 500	
Office Secretary	£ 5 500	
		£55 000

Commissions (based on sales of £4 000 000)

Branch Manager (0.1%)	£ 4 000	
Salesmen (0.9%)	£36 000	
		£40 000

Travel and Entertainment
(Averaging £25 per sales person per day for
an annual average of 225 days per sales person)   £28 125

Office Expenses
Rent, utilities, supplies, etc.   £ 7 500

Total branch expenditure   £130 625

In preparing a budget for the next 12 months it is anticipated that:
(a) the branch manager's salary will rise by £1 000;
(b) each sales person's base salary will remain unchanged, but the commission rate
will increase to 1.0%;
(c) the office secretary's salary will be increased by £60 per month;
(d) two additional sales people are to be employed (on the same terms as the
existing sales force);
(e) the sales quota for the branch will be £5 000 000;
(f) travel and entertainment expenses are likely to increase by 4% per sales
person-day;
(g) a special promotional campaign will be undertaken at a cost of £12 000;
(h) the office expenses will rise by 5%.

Required
(i) Prepare the 1986–7 budget for the Bamford sales office.
(ii) Assuming the actual results for 1986–7 are in line with the budget, comment on
the relative performance in 1985–6 and 1986–7 of the Bamford sales office.
(Institute of Marketing)

6 Sad Story Ltd is suffering from a world-wide depression in the market for its
products. At a level of 70% of capacity, production is exceeding sales and a more
realistic forecast for the next period is a 50% level of activity. The following data has
already been prepared.

	Level of activity		
	60%	70%	80%
Direct Materials	37 800	44 100	50 400
Direct Wages	16 200	18 900	21 600
Production Overhead	37 600	41 200	44 800
Administration Overhead	31 500	31 500	31 500
Selling and Distribution Overhead	42 300	44 100	45 900
Total Cost	165 400	179 800	194 200

Profit is 20% of selling price.

Required:
(a) A Budget in Marginal Costing format for a 50% level of activity, showing the
resultant profit or loss.
(b) A brief explanation of the means by which the 50% forecast level of activity will
have been arrived at.

(c) Further advice on the implications of operating at a 50% level of activity and some ideas to enable an improved level of activity to be achieved, both in the short-term and in the long-term.

(Association of Business Executives)

7 You have estimated the following figures from the books of Acas Ltd.

Production (Units)

	1984				1985			
Nov	Dec	Jan	Feb	Mar	Apr	May	June
800	900	1 000	1 100	1 300	1 400	1 500	1 200

- Raw Material costs £40 per unit, paid for two months before it is used in production.
- Direct Labour costs £30 per unit and is paid for in the month in which units are produced.
- Other Variable Expenses cost £20 per unit, paid as to 3/4 in the same month as production and 1/4 in the month following production.
- Fixed Expenses are £10 000 per month, paid monthly.
- Sales (Units)

	1984		1985
Oct	Nov	Dec	Jan
800	900	700	1 000

- Selling price is £120 per unit, received three months after sale.
- Plant is to be acquired and paid for in April 1985 – £80 000. Cash Balance at 1 January 1985 – £320 000.

Prepare a Cash Forecast for each of the months of January to April, 1985.
Present your statement in £000, using one decimal point to represent £00.

(Association of Business Executives)

8 Write short, explanatory notes on:
  (a) budget committee;
  (b) budget review period;
  (c) budget manual.

9 A new company has gathered the following information for the six months from 1 July to 31 December 1987.

(a) Sales (in units) £40 per unit.

July	Aug	Sept	Oct	Nov	Dec
200	300	200	400	300	400

(b) Production will be at the rate of 300 units per month for the *whole* of the six months.

(c) Fixed overhead costs will be £3 000 per month payable in the month after production.

(d) Variable overhead costs will be £15 per unit produced payable in the month of production.

(e) Direct wages will be £5 per unit produced.

(f) Equipment costing £10 000 will be purchased in August and paid for in September.

(g) Direct Materials will be £8 per unit and suppliers will be paid in the month following purchases.

(h) All sales are on one month credit.

(i) Initial balance at bank on 1 July 1987 will be £10 000.

You are required to:

(a) Prepare a Cash Budget for July–December 1987.

(b) Write a short report commenting on the Cash Budget.

(Inst. of Commercial Management – modified)

7 Standard costing and variance analysis

■ INTRODUCTION

Standard costing is a well established technique, widely practised throughout all the manufacturing industries. Students should note that although in many accounting text-books budgetary control is dealt with separately from standard costing and variance analysis, the two are, in fact, integral parts of the same system of control.

Standard costs are costs which are *predetermined prior to the budget period*. They are normative costs in that they set norms of operational performance required by management. Also, it should be noted, standard costs – because they indicate what the various cost levels should be – provide a useful yardstick for evaluating current actual performance.

■ VARIANCES

The differences between actual costs and standard costs are known as variances; and the calculation, classification and evaluation of variances is known as *variance analysis*. Variances may be of different kinds. From the point of view of the effect they have on profits, we distinguish *favourable variances* (which increase profits) and *adverse variances* (which decrease profits). From the point of view of the manager's ability to influence actual costs, we may distinguish *controllable variances* (for which full responsibility should be accepted) and *uncontrollable variances* which, regretfully, do not lend themselves to corrective action by management.

Although there is a fair degree of uniformity in the kinds of variances used in various industries, in practice it will be found that many variances are specific to particular industries only. The list of variances given below consists of variances which are basic and in common use. Let us now look at some examples illustrating the calculation of variances.

EXAMPLE 1

	£
Standard Sales: 1 000 units @ £10.00 per unit	10 000
Actual Sales: 1 200 units @ £9.00 per unit	10 800

It is clear that the overall difference between standard sales and actual sales is due to two reasons: (a) larger than standard number of units sold and (b) lower price per unit. We may explain the difference between standard and actual sales as follows:

	£
Standard Sales: 1 000 units @ £10.00 per units	10 000
add Volume Variance – 200 units @ £10.00 per unit	2 000
	12 000
less Price Variance – 1 200 units @ £1.00 per unit	1 200
Actual Sales	10 800

Students should note that the volume variance is calculated at the standard price. Any difference between the standard and actual price is included in the price variance.

EXAMPLE 2

	£
Standard Cost of Materials –	
100 units – 500 kg @ £2.00 per kg	1,000
Actual Cost of Materials –	
110 units – 570 kg @ £1.90 per kg	1,083

The difference of £83 between the standard and actual cost is due to three reasons: (a) larger than standard output; (b) lower cost of raw materials and (c) excessive usage of materials. We may reconcile the standard and actual cost as follows:

	£
Standard Cost of 100 units –	
500 kg @ £2.00 per kg	1,000
add Volume Variance – 50 kg @ £2.00 per kg	100
Standard Cost of Actual Output	1,100
add Usage Variance – 20 kg @ £2.00 per kg	40
	1,140
less Price Variance – 570 kg @ £0.10 per kg	57
Actual Cost of Materials	1 083

The standard quantity of materials for the actual output of 110 units is 550 kg. As 570 kg was used, the 20 kg represent excessive usage of materials.

EXAMPLE 3

	£
Standard Cost of Direct Labour –	
100 units – 1 000 hrs @ £5.00 per hr	5 000
Actual cost of Direct Labour –	
120 units – 1 320 @ £5.20 per hr	6 864

The difference between the standard and actual cost here is due to three reasons:
    (a) larger than standard output;
    (b) higher than standard rate of hourly pay;
    (c) excessive time taken to produce the actual output.
Our reconciliation is as follows:

	£
Standard Cost of 100 units –	
1 000 hrs @ £5.00 per hr	5 000
add Volume Variance – 200 hrs @ £5.00 per hr	1 000
Standard Cost of Actual Output	6 000
add Rate of Pay Variance – 1320 hrs @ £0.20 per hr	264
	6 264
add Efficiency Variance – £120 hrs @ £5.00 per hr	600
Actual Cost of Direct Labour	6 864

■ A WORKED EXAMPLE

The A-n-B Co. Ltd manufactures and sells two products, A and B. Set out below are the standard figures in respect of the first quarter of 19...

STANDARD

	£	£
Product A – 10 000 units @ £30.00 per unit	300 000	
Product B – 20 000 units @ £15.00 per unit	300 000	600 000
less Prod. A Material X 20 000 kg @ £4.00 per kg	80 000	
Prod. A Material Y 10 000 kg @ £2.00 per kg	20 000	
Prod. B Material X 10 000 kg @ £4.00 per kg	40 000	
Prod. B Material Y 30 000 kg @ £2.00 per kg	60 000	
Prod. A Dir. Lab. 10 000 hrs @ £4.00 per hr	40 000	
Prod. B Dir. Lab. 20 000 hrs @ £4.00 per hr	80 000	
Prod. A V'ble O'head – 10 000 units @ £1.00 per unit	10 000	
Prod. B V'ble O'head – 20 000 units @ £2.00 per unit	40 000	
Adm. Sell. & Distr. Expenses	170 000	540 000
Standard Net Profit		60 000

At the end of the first quarter the following actual figures became available.

ACTUAL

	£	£
Product A – 11 000 units @ £31.00 per unit	341 000	
Product B – 18 000 units @ £16.00 per unit	288 000	629 000
less Prod. A Material X 23 000 kg @ £4.20 per kg	96 600	
Prod. A Material Y 11 200 kg @ £1.80 per kg	20 160	
Prod. B Material X 9 200 kg @ £4.20 per kg	38 640	
Prod. B Material Y 26 000 kg @ £1.80 per kg	46 800	
Prod. A Dir. Lab. 10 800 hrs @ £4.10 per hr	44 280	
Prod. B Dir. Lab. 18 400 hrs @ £4.10 per hr	75 440	
Prod. A V'ble O'head – 11 000 units @ £0.80 per unit	8 800	
Prod. B V'ble O'head – 18 000 units @ £2.10 per unit	37 800	
Adm. Sell. & Distr. Expenses	180 000	548 520
Actual Net Profit		80 480

Our next task is to calculate the variances in respect of each element of cost and reconcile the actual and standard net profit.

Calculation of Variances:

Prod. A – St. Sales	£300 000	Prod. B – St. Sales	£300 000
add Vol. V. 1 000 @ £30.00	30 000	*add* Price V. 18 000 @ £1.00	18 000
	330 000		318 000
add Price V. 11 000 @ £1.00	11 000	*less* Vol. V. 2 000 @ £15.00	30 000
Actual Sales	341 000	Actual Sales	288 000

Prod. A Mat X – St. Cost	£80 000	Prod. B Mat X – St. Cost	£40 000
add Vol. V. 2 000 kg @ £4.00	8 000	*add* Price V. 9 200 @ £0.20	1 840
	88 000		41 840
add Usage V. 1 000 kg @ £4.00	4 000	*add* Usage V. 200 @ £4.00	800
	92 000		42 640
add Price V. 23 000 @ £0.20	4 600	*less* Vol. V. 1 000 @ £4.00	4000
Actual Cost	96 600	Actual Cost	38 640

Prod. A Mat Y, St. Cost	£20 000	Prod. B Mat Y, St. Cost	£60 000
add Vol. V. 1 000 @ £2.00	2 000	*less* Price V. 26 000 @ £0.20	5 200
	22 000		54 800
add Usage V. 200 @ £2.00	400	*less* Vol. V. 3 000 @ £2.00	6 000
	22 400		48 800
less Price V. 11 200 @ £0.20	2 240	*less* Usage V. 1 000 @ £2.00	2 000
Actual Cost	20 160	Actual Cost	46 800

Prod. A Dir. Lab. St. Cost	£40 000	Prod. B Dir. Lab. St. Cost	£80 000
add Vol. V. 1 000 @ £4.00	4 000	*add* R/Pay V. 18 400 @ £0.10	1 840
	44 000		81 000
add R/Pay V. 10 800 @ £0.10	1 080	*add* Efficiency V. 400 @ £4.00	1 600
	45 080		83 440
less Efficiency V. 200 @ £4.00	800	*less* Vol. V. 2 000 @ £4.00	8 000
Actual Cost	44 280	Actual Cost	75 440

Prod. A V'ble O'head St. Cost	£10 000	Prod. B V'ble O'head St. Cost	£40 000
add Vol. V. 1 000 @ £1.00	1 000	*add* Price V. 18 000 @ £0.10	1 800
	11 000		41 800
less Price V. 11 000 @ £0.20	2 200	*less* Vol. V. 2 000 @ £2.00	4 000
Actual Cost	8 800	Actual Cost	37 800

Adm. Sell. & Distr. Exps. – St. Cost	£170 000
add Expenditure V.	10 000
Actual Cost	180 000

Let us explain in more detail some of the above calculations before we proceed further.

Sales:
Students should note that the volume variance is calculated at the standard price. The price variance is based on the actual volume – in the case of Product A, all 11 000 units attracted an extra £1.00.

Materials:
Actual output of Product A was 10 per cent more than standard and, therefore, 22 000 kg of Material X should have been used. As 23 000 kg were used, the excess of 1 000 kg represents excessive usage, shown as a usage variance.

Direct Labour:
Rate of pay variances are in the same category as materials price variances. The efficiency variance of £800 in respect of Product A results from the hours saved in production. As actual output was 10 per cent more than standard 11 000 hours should have been worked whilst the actual number of hours was 10 800.

Adm. Sell & Distr. Expenses:
We are not sure about the causes of the £10 000 variance and, therefore, describe it as an 'expenditure' variance.

It is worth noting that whilst the overall variance between the standard and actual net profit is £20 480, the sum total of all the variances is (£93 440 + £72 960) £166 400. Very fortunately the favourable variances have more than offset the negative variances. Our method of presenting the reconciliation here is quite typical in that we have started with the standard net profit, added the favourable variances, deducted the adverse variances and thus arrived at the actual net profit. Other methods of presentation are possible depending on individual preferences.

Reconciliation

	£	£
Standard Net Profit		60 000
add Prod. A Sales Vol. Var.	30 000	
Prod. A Sales Price V.	11 000	
Prod. B Sales Price V.	18 000	
Prod. A Mat. Y Price V.	2 240	
Prod. B Mat. X Vol. V.	4 000	
Prod. B Mat. Y Price. V.	5 200	
Prod. B Mat. Y Vol. V.	6 000	
Prod. B Mat. Y Usage V.	2 000	
Prod. A Lab. Eff. V.	800	
Prod. B Dir. Lab. Vol. V.	8 000	
Prod. A V'ble O'head Price C.	2 200	
Prod. B V'ble O'head Vol. V.	4 000	93 440
		153 440
less Prod. B Sales Vol. V.	30 000	
Prod. A Mat. X Vol. V.	8 000	
Prod. A Mat. X Usage V.	4 000	
Prod. A Mat. X Price V.	4 600	
Prod. A Mat. Y Vol. V.	2 000	
Prod. A Mat. Y Usage V.	400	
Prod. B Mat. X Price V.	1 840	
Prod. B Mat. X Usage V.	800	
Prod. A Dir. Lab. Vol. V.	4 000	
Prod. A Dir. Lab. R/Pay V.	1 080	
Prod. B Dir. Lab. R/Pay V.	1 840	
Prod. B Dir. Lab. Eff. V.	1 600	
Prod. A V'ble O'head Vol. V.	1 000	
Prod. B V'ble O'head Price V.	1 800	
Adm. Sell. & Distr. Exps. Expend. V.	10 000	72 960
Actual Net Profit		80 480

■ SELF ASSESSMENT QUESTIONS

1   The manager of the Finishing Department has been provided with the following information relating to performance for April 1985:

Actual cost of materials used	£37 884
Actual quantity of materials used	49 200 kilos

Actual wages paid to direct workers   £78 440
Actual hours of direct labour   21 200 hours
Actual production   20 000 units

Extracts from the Master budget for the Finishing Department give:

Standard time per unit   1 hour
Standard wage per direct labour hour   £3.50
Standard quantity of material per unit   2.5 kilos
Standard cost of material per unit   80p

Required:
(a) A variance analysis.
(b) An explanation, for a non-accountant such as the manager of the Finishing Department, of the meaning of each of the variances calculated.

(Association of Business Executives)

2 Write short, explanatory notes on:
(a) standard costs;
(b) favourable variances;
(c) adverse variances;
(d) controllable variances;
(e) uncontrollable variances

3 Technical Toys plc has operated a standard costing system for some time. It produces only one product, the Transformer Ship and the standard costs for the ship for the current period are reproduced below:

	£ (per unit)
Direct labour 2 hours at £4.50 per hour	9.00
Direct material 4 lbs at £7.50 per lb.	30.00
Variable overhead 2 hours at £1.50 per hour	3.00
Fixed overheads 2 hours at £3.00 per hour	6.00
	48.00

The budgeted fixed overheads for the period were £30 000 based on a budgeted level of production for the period of 5 000 units. The standard selling price for the ship was £75.00.

Recently the actual results for the period became available and are shown below:

	£	£
Sales (4 700 units)		361 900
Direct labour: 9 750 hours	46 310	
Direct material: 24 000 lbs	174 000	
Variable overhead:	16 550	
Fixed overhead:	33 000	269 860
Profit		92 040

Calculate cost and sales variances for the period in question.

(Association of Business Executives)

4 (a) The following data relates to product X for last month:

	Budget	Actual	Variance
Sales	£990 000	£800 000	£190 000
Units Sold	110 000	100 000	
Unit Price	£9.00	£8.00	

Explain the variance of £190 000

(b) How might a manager establish the significance of variances? Why is it important that he/she should?

(Institute of Marketing)

5 The Trio Trading Company sells three products, X, Y and Z. At the end of Month 7 the following figures are available.

	Budget			Actual		
	Units	Price	Value	Units	Price	Value
Product X	10 000	4.40	44 000	11 000	4.20	46 200
Product Y	8 000	8.20	65 600	7 600	8.40	63 840
Product Z	6 000	7.00	42 000	6 600	7.20	47 520

You are required to calculate appropriate variances and reconcile actual and budgeted sales for Month 7; and to set out your figures in the form of a simple tabulated report, addressed to the Sales Manager of the company.

(Schiller International University)

6 The Vicmarks Production Company uses a standard costing system. The standard cost of one of its products is:

  5 units of Material X at £0.70 per unit
 10 units of Material Y at £1.10 per unit

  6 hours of Grade A labour at £4.00 per hour
  2 hours of Grade B labour at £3.20 per hour

The actual cost of 1 000 items of production was as follows:

  5 500 units of Material X at a cost of £3 575
  9 700 units of Material Y at a cost of £11 640

  5 750 hours of Grade A labour at a cost of £24 150
  2 100 hours of Grade B labour at a cost of £6 405

You are required to:
(a) Compute the appropriate labour and material cost variances.
(b) Suggest possible explanations for the variances.
(c) Briefly describe the major benefits of standard costing.

(Institute of Commercial Management)

8 | Financial statement analysis

■ INTRODUCTION

The aim of the present chapter is twofold: (a) to explain the principal ratios in use throughout industry and commerce and (b) show how such ratios are used in the process of analysing and interpreting financial statements – profit and loss accounts and balance sheets.

Students should appreciate that bare, dry figures – however accurate – cannot tell the whole truth. And so when we prepare the annual accounts and show that last year's sales amounted to £5 000 000, then this in itself means little. If, however, we show last year's sales of £5 000 000 and additionally give the corresponding figure of sales for the year before, say £4 000 000, then we are beginning to supply information which is meaningful. Similarly if we show in our Profit and Loss A/c a net profit of £200 000 then again this, in itself, means only little. The figure only begins to acquire some meaning if it is related to some other relevant figure. And so if we relate the current net profit of £200 000 to last year's net profit of, say, £150 000 or budgeted net profit of, say, £180 000 or sales revenue of, say, £1 000 000 then – and only then – are we supplying information whose significance is intelligible.

From the above examples it will be appreciated that meaningful figures can only be provided where there is some point of reference or comparison – normally where one figure or quantity is shown or expressed in relation to some other relevant figure or quantity. It is in this context of comparisons that ratios are of particular value.

A ratio is a statistical device which measures the relationship between two quantities. Thus where there are 20 students and 5 teachers, we may say that the ratio of students to teachers is 20:5 or 4:1. If we had 17 students and 5 teachers it would be more convenient to divide the number of students by the number of teachers and express the relationship as 3·4. Also some ratios are, in practice, shown as percentages. Where there is a net profit of £130 000 and sales amount to £870 000, it would not be meaningful to show a ratio of 87:13 and the accountant would express this in the form of a percentage as 14.9%.

It is possible in most situations to calculate a large number of ratios. Such ratios may be classified in several different ways.

An *accounting ratio* is one which is calculated by reference to the annual accounts, i.e. Profit and Loss Account and Balance Sheet. Net profit expressed as a ratio of net sales and net profit expressed as a ratio of capital would both be calculated by reference to the final accounts and, therefore, classified as accounting ratios.

A *balance sheet ratio* is one which is calculated by reference to the Balance Sheet. The relationship between current assets and current liabilities – known as the current ratio – is in this category. A *profit and loss ratio* is one calculated by reference to the Profit and Loss Account. Both the gross profit ratio and the net profit ratio are profit and loss ratios.

Operating ratios are specific to various industries, and are intended to ensure the daily/weekly progress of the business concerned. For example, in the building trade it is possible to calculate the daily/weekly number of bricks laid per worker. In a supermarket we may calculate the sales volume per square metre of shop floor or per employee.

Whilst some ratios are concerned with the profitability of the enterprise, others measure its liquidity. Examples of *profitability ratios* are gross profit ratio, net profit ratio and return on capital. Examples of *liquidity ratios* are current ratio and acid test ratio.

Our discussion of ratios which now follows deals with the various ratios under the headings of 'profitability ratios' and 'liquidity ratios'. All businesses must, in order to survive, be both profitable and adequately liquid; and it is these two aspects that students are frequently expected to discuss in examinations. It is hoped that the classification of ratios adopted here will promote the right approach and help students tackle questions on ratio analysis and interpretation of accounts.

■ PROFITABILITY RATIOS

Gross profit ratio

This measures the relationship between gross profit and net sales. The formula for calculating this ratio (invariably expressed as a percentage) is:

$$\frac{\text{Gross Profit} \quad £400\,000}{\text{Net Sales} \quad £1\,000\,000} \times 100 = 40\%$$

Students should note that the gross profit ratio will differ very considerably from one type of business operation to another. Wholesalers operate at lower gross profit margins than retailers. Within retailing there are also considerable differences from one type of operation to another, e.g. gross profit margins on food products are generally lower than those on luxury goods.

Net profit ratio

This measures the relationship between net profit and net sales. The formula for calculating this ratio is:

$$\frac{\text{Net Profit} \quad £130\,000}{\text{Net Sales} \quad £1\,000\,000} \times 100 = 13.0\%$$

It is not easy to suggest what constitutes a satisfactory net profit ratio as this is necessarily dependent on general business conditions, the type of business operation, etc. It is important to remember that the net profit ratio is a measure of the relative operating efficiency of the business from one accounting period to another.

Return on capital

This is also described as return on capital employed or return on net worth; it measures the relationship between net profit and the capital of the business and constitutes a most important measure of profitability. The formula here is:

$$\frac{\text{Net Profit} \quad £130\,000}{\text{Capital} \quad £800\,000} \times 100 = 16.3\%$$

Whilst in the case of the sole trader all the capital will be provided by one person, the capital of a large limited company will normally consist of different types of finance obtained from different sources. It is for this reason that we have to enlarge on the above basic definition of return on capital.

A large limited company may have a balance sheet structured as follows:

Balance Sheet

(a) Ordinary Shares	XXX			
(b) Preference Shares	XXX	Fixed Assets	XXX	
(c) Debentures	XXX			
(d) Current Liabilities	XXX	Current Assets	XXX	

Students should appreciate that the left-hand side shows where the finance has come from. The right-hand side shows how such finance has been invested in the fixed and current assets of the business. Quite obviously where, as in this particular case, there are four sources of capital, we may have four different definitions of capital. Therefore when we calculate return on capital we may define it as:

(a) return on ordinary shareholders' (equity) capital;
(b) return on total shareholders' capital;
(c) return on long-term capital;
(d) return on total capital.

Each of the above definitions of capital requires an appropriate definition of profit, as follows:

(a) If we define capital as ordinary share capital (plus any reserves), the relevant definition of profit is the sum of ordinary dividends plus undistributed profits. In other words, we must exclude preference dividends and any debenture interest.

(b) If we define capital as total shareholders' capital, we must define profit as the total of dividends paid plus undistributed profits.

(c) If we define capital as long-term capital, the correct definition of profit is the total of all dividends, debenture interest and undistributed profits.

(d) Finally, if we define capital as total capital, the definition of profit is the same as for long-term capital – simply because the existence of current liabilities does not present a claim on business profits.

It is not easy to say which of the four definitions should normally be used, as circumstances will vary somewhat from one situation to another. What is very important, however, is that the same definition of capital should be used consistently from one accounting period to another.

■ LIQUIDITY RATIOS

The term 'liquidity' relates to the availability of cash and liquid resources and the organization's ability to pay its short-term debts. A business is, therefore, said to be liquid if it has adequate cash, debtors and stocks in relation to its current commitments (creditors, accrued expenses, bank overdrafts, etc.).

Current ratio

This measures the relationship between current assets and current liabilities. Where current assets amount to £50 000 and current liabilities are £20 000, the current ratio is:

$$\frac{\text{Current Assets} \quad £50\,000}{\text{Current Liabilities} \quad £20\,000} = 2.5$$

For a long time, and until recently, accountants used to say that a sound current ratio is 2:1 (or 2.0). It is now recognized, however, that different types of business operation result in different – indeed very different – current ratios in different industries. As a general rule manufacturing and trading organizations require heavy stocks of raw materials and finished goods to support their operations; and in such circumstances current ratios of 2.0 to 5.0 are not uncommon. Thus dealers in furniture, jewellers and all kinds of wholesalers maintain substantial stocks which result in above-average current assets. On the other hand, hotels, leisure centres, transport undertakings, etc. do not require huge stocks for operational purposes; and in such businesses current ratios may well be as low as 1.2 to 2.0. Students should, therefore, realize that what is right and proper in one case may well be wholly improper in another.

The difference between current assets and current liabilities is described as *working capital*, which in the above example is:

	£
Current Assets	50 000
less Current Liabilities	20 000
Working Capital	30 000

Working capital is that part of the total capital of the business which is used to support its day-to-day operations such as payment of creditors, wages, salaries and other operational outgoings. It should be distinguished from the permanent capital which consists of land, buildings, plant, equipment, etc. – all of which items must be acquired before the commencement of operations.

Acid test ratio

This is also described as the 'quick assets ratio' and measures the relationship between *liquid assets* and current liabilities. Liquid assets are cash and current assets which are easily convertible into cash. Debtors are normally regarded as liquid but stocks are not. Let us look at an example.

Balance Sheet

		£			£
Capital		190 000	Fixed Assets		170 000
Current Liabilities			*Current Assets*		
Creditors	7 000		Stocks	25 000	
Accrued Expenses	3 000	10 000	Debtors	3 000	
			Cash	2 000	30 000
		200 000			200 000

In the above example the current ratio is 3:1 (or 3.0) which in many types of business operation would be regarded as quite satisfactory. The acid test ratio, however, is only 0.5:1.0 (or 0.5) which is far from being satisfactory, as for every £1.00 owed to suppliers and other parties we have only £0.50 in cash and liquid resources. The acid test ratio is, therefore, a more stringent measure of liquidity.

Rate of stock turnover

The rate of stock turnover measures the speed with which stocks move through the business. As a general rule, a high rate of stock turnover is an indication that low stocks are kept in relation to the sales volume; and, conversely, a low rate of stock turnover tends to indicate that high stocks are being kept. The formula for calculating the rate of stock turnover is:

$$\frac{\text{Cost of Sales} \quad £120\,000}{\text{Average Stock at Cost} \quad £10\,000} = 12 \text{ (times)}$$

Average stock for this purpose is generally taken to be the average of opening and closing stocks. Our rate of stock turnover in the above example indicates that the average or typical stock is turned over (re-purchased or re-sold) twelve times a year. Consequently the average stock held in this business is sufficient for one month's operation.

Rates of stock turnover vary from one industry to another. A dealer in furniture will need very substantial stocks for effective operations and may have a stock turnover of only 4–5 a year. A fishmonger, on the other hand, will replace his stocks several times a week and may have a rate of stock turnover in excess of 100. In the case of a particular business a downward trend in the rate of stock turnover may be an indication that excessively high stocks are being accumulated. Unjustifiably high stocks have the effect of reducing the acid test ratio; also money invested in idle stocks is a poor investment and particularly so if the stock is one of perishable goods.

Average collection period

This measures the period of credit extended to the debtors or the speed with which debts are collected from the customers of the business. If a business sells, one year, goods on credit to the value of £520 000, and at the end of the year debtors amount to £80 000, the average collection period will be as follows:

Credit Sales – per annum	£520 000
No. of Weeks	52
Credit Sales – per week	£ 10 000

As debtors amount to £80 000, they represent 8 weeks' credit sales, which in many situations would be regarded as unsatisfactory, as too long a period of credit is extended to customers. In order to control the collection of debts many organizations appoint a credit controller, who will not only investigate the credit worthiness of potential customers but also keep an eye on the cash collected from customers from one week to another.

Average payment period

This measures the period of credit received from the suppliers. It is calculated in a similar manner to the average collection period. Thus, where annual credit purchases amount to £260 000 and creditors at the end of the year amount to

£20 000, the average payment period is:

$$\frac{\text{Creditors} \quad £20\ 000}{\text{Weekly Credit Purchases} \quad £5\ 000} = 4 \text{ weeks}$$

An average payment period of 4 weeks indicates that suppliers' statements are paid promptly; and presumably that cash discounts are not lost through dilatory settlement of suppliers' accounts.

■ OPERATING RATIOS

Accounting ratios are calculated by reference to the Profit and Loss Account and Balance Sheet; and necessarily, therefore, cover long periods of time. Operating ratios, on the other hand, are prepared frequently – daily and weekly – by reference to various control documents. The main advantage of operating ratios is that they provide an immediate indication of the progress of the business – almost on a daily basis. Frequently, therefore, managers will pay more attention to the operating ratios as these have an obvious and direct relevance to the operations they control than the accounting ratios, many of which can only be calculated after the preparation of the annual or half-yearly accounts.

Operating ratios are specific to particular industries. In retailing organizations it is usual to calculate each week ratios such as:

- sales per employee;
- sales per square metre of floor space;
- cash taken per cashier;
- cash taken per opening hour, etc.

Trading organizations will calculate ratios in respect of:

- sales revenue per sales representative;
- number and value of new orders received each week;
- value of goods delivered per available vehicle, etc.

Hotels will calculate:

- each day/week their room occupancy (rooms sold as a percentage of available rooms);
- average amounts spent by guests on food and drinks, etc.

A food manufacturing company will calculate:

- the daily/weekly tonnage of food processed;
- total output in relation to existing capacity;
- output per employee, etc.

All such operating ratios are regarded by managers as critical indicators of current performance; and it is the duty of every management accountant to pay sufficient attention to such ratios.

In the example shown below for the Mercurial Food Market, we detail a large number of operating ratios which would be supplied on a weekly basis in large retailing operations. Our Weekly Sales Report shows a great deal of useful information on matters such as: sales mix; weekly pattern of business; the incidence of the sales volume per shop assistant and per cashier from one day to another.

Quite clearly from the store manager's point of view all such ratios are of direct relevance in that they: (a) give a clear, detailed picture of the weekly sales revenue and (b) suggest how he or she should respond to the weekly pattern of business in terms of the deployment of staff. It is clear in this particular case that, although the number of staff is larger at the end of the week, this adjustment in the labour force is rather sluggish.

MERCURIAL FOOD MARKET
Weekly Sales Report for .....

	Mon	Tue	Wed	Thu	Fri	Sat	Total
Sales mix – £	£	£	£	£	£	£	£
Meat and fish	3 500	4 000	4 500	7 000	8 500	9 500	37 000
Fruit and vegetables	2 000	2 500	3 000	4 500	5 500	6 000	23 500
Dairy produce	1 500	2 000	2 500	3 500	5 000	5 500	20 000
Groceries	3 000	3 500	4 000	6 000	8 000	9 000	33 500
	10 000	12 000	14 000	21 000	27 000	30 000	114 000
Sales mix – %	%	%	%	%	%	%	%
Meat and fish	35.0	33.3	32.1	33.3	31.5	31.7	32.5
Fruit and vegetables	20.0	20.8	21.4	21.4	20.4	20.0	20.6
Dairy produce	15.0	16.7	17.9	16.7	18.5	18.3	17.5
Groceries	30.0	29.2	28.6	28.6	29.6	30.0	29.4
	100.0	100.0	100.0	100.0	100.0	100.0	100.0
No. of customers	495	593	690	974	1 203	1 333	5 288
	£	£	£	£	£	£	£
Sales per customer	20.20	20.24	20.29	21.56	22.44	22.50	21.56
No. of shop assistants	15	15	15	20	20	30	115
	£	£	£	£	£	£	£
Sales per shop assistant	667	800	933	1 050	1 350	1 000	991
Customers per shop assistant	33	40	46	49	60	44	46
No. of cashiers	7	7	8	8	10	10	50
	£	£	£	£	£	£	£
Sales per cashier	1 429	1 714	1 750	1 625	2 700	3 000	2 280
Customers per cashier	71	85	86	122	120	133	106

EXAMPLE 1

Set out below are the annual accounts of New Horizons Ltd. You are required to calculate the following ratios and comment on the results, indicating what other information you would require.

(a) Gross profit percentage;
(b) Net profit percentage;
(c) Return on total assets;
(d) Quick assets ratio;
(e) Current ratio;
(f) Debtors collection period;
(g) Stock turnover.

Debtors : = 770,000 / 59

Balance Sheet at 30 April 1985

	£000
Share capital	450
Retained profits	240
	690
12% Debentures	700
Trade Creditors	620
Proposed Dividend	45
	£2 055
Fixed Assets net of Depreciation	875
Stock	310
Debtors	770
Bank Balance	100
	£2 055
Sales for the Year	£3 100 000
Gross profit	1 725 000
Expenses	805 000
Depreciation	250 000

(Institute of Marketing – modified)

SOLUTION

(a) Gross Profit %:

$$\frac{\text{Gross Profit} \quad \text{£1 725 000}}{\text{Sales} \quad \text{£3 100 000}} \times 100 = 55.6\%$$

It would be helpful to know what kind of product(s) the company is selling. The gross profit of 55.6% appears to be very satisfactory; indeed it is not often one sees such a high profit ratio in practice.

(b) Net Profit %:
Net profit before tax is, in this case:

Gross Profit		£1 725 000
less Expenses	£805 000	
Depreciation	250 000	£1 055 000
Net Profit		670 000

$$\frac{\text{Net Profit} \quad £670\ 000}{\text{Sales} \quad £3\ 100\ 000} \times 100 = 21.6\%$$

A net profit on sales of 21.6% would probably be regarded as quite adequate by most companies. It would help, however, to have additional information on how charges for depreciation were calculated and on the composition of the total expenses of £805 000.

(c) Return on Total Assets:
Students should note that total assets may be expressed as the total of fixed assets and current assets (£875 000 + £1 180 000 = £2 055 000) or as the total of: share capital, retained profits, debentures and current liabilities (£450 000 + £240 000 + £700 000 + £665 000 = £2 055 000).

$$\frac{\text{Net Profit} \quad £670\ 000}{\text{Total Assets} \quad £2\ 055\ 000} \times 100 = 32.6\%$$

A return on total assets of 32.6% seems very satisfactory indeed. It would be interesting, however, to know what returns on total assets were achieved by the company during the last few years prior to the accounting year under review, i.e. 1984–85. Also it would help if information were available on the method of valuation of fixed assets.

(d) Quick Assets Ratio:
Quick assets, or liquid assets, consist here of debtors and the bank balance – a total of £870 000. Therefore:

$$\frac{\text{Liquid Assets} \quad £870\ 000}{\text{Current Liabilities} \quad £665\ 000} = 1.3$$

For every £1 owed to trade creditors and shareholders the company has £1.30 in cash and debtors. This appears to be quite satisfactory.

(e) Current Ratio:

$$\frac{\text{Current Assets} \quad £1\ 180\ 000}{\text{Current Liabilities} \quad £665\ 000} = 1.8$$

A current ratio of 1.8 may or may not be satisfactory depending on the type of business operation. One should, therefore, attach more importance to the quick assets (or acid test) ratio.

(f) Debtors Collection Period:
Let us assume that the company sells on credit only.

Sales per annum	£3 100 000
No. of weeks	52
Sales per week	£59 615

Therefore:

$$\frac{\text{Debtors} \quad £770\ 000}{\text{Weekly Credit Sales} \quad £59\ 615} = 12.9 \text{ weeks}$$

The company appears to be extending a very long period of credit to its customers. Comparative figures for previous periods would certainly help.

(g) Stock Turnover:
We do not know the opening stock; and have to assume that the closing stock of £310 000 is typical or average. The cost of sales is calculated here by deducting the gross profit from the sales revenue. Hence:

Sales	£3 100 000
less Gross Profit	1 725 000
Cost of Sales	1 375 000

Therefore:

$$\frac{\text{Cost of Sales} \quad £1\ 375\ 000}{\text{Stock} \quad £310\ 000} = 4.4$$

A rate of stock turnover of 4.4 seems quite low and it would help to have information on the nature of business conducted by the company.

EXAMPLE 2

The following are the results of Determined Productions Ltd, who are weavers of small carpets and rugs, selling them to retailers and by mail order.

Summarized Profit and Loss Account for year ended 31 December 1984

	£000s
Sales	1 600
Cost of Goods Sold	1 200
Gross Profit	400
Expenses and Depreciation	300
Net Profit	100
Ordinary Share Dividend	60
Retained Profit	40

Balance Sheet as at 31 December 1984
Assets: £000s
    Land and Building (at cost)   310
    Equipment (at cost, less depreciation to date)   250
    Stock   120
    Trade Debtors   200
    Bank Balance   20
                                                        ―――
                                                        900
                                                        ===

Financed by:
    Ordinary Share Capital   600
    Retained Profits   200
    Trade Creditors   100
                                                        ―――
                                                        900
                                                        ===

Required:
Calculate six ratios which you consider relevant and explain their importance to the Managing Director of Determined Productions Ltd.

                                             (Association of Business Executives)

SOLUTION

Let us choose three ratios measuring profitability and three measuring liquidity.

Profitability
Net Profit Ratio:

$$\frac{\text{Net Profit} \quad £100\,000}{\text{Sales} \quad £1\,600\,000} \times 100 = \underline{6.3\%}$$

The net profit ratio measures the relative operating efficiency of the business from one accounting period to another. A high net profit ratio suggests that, in relation to the current sales volume, costs are adequately controlled. A low net profit ratio, as in this case, may be an indication of insufficient gross profit margins and/or a high level of expenses.

Gross Profit Ratio:

$$\frac{\text{Gross Profit} \quad £400\,000}{\text{Sales} \quad £1\,600\,000} \times 100 = \underline{25.0\%}$$

Gross profit is the difference between sales and cost of sales; and the gross profit ratio measures the profits made on the buying and selling of goods – before deduction of other operating expenses. A gross profit ratio of 25% means that every time we sell goods (carpets in this case) to the value of £10 000, our gross profit margin will be (25% of £10 000) £2 500.

Return on Total Assets:

$$\frac{\text{Net Profit} \quad £100\,000}{\text{Total Assets} \quad £900\,000} \times 100 = \underline{11.1\%}$$

Total assets are all the fixed assets and current assets at the disposal of management, which are used to produce a satisfactory profit for the business. Such assets typically represent a substantial amount of finance which, if invested elsewhere, would produce a given amount of profit. It is the management's responsibility, therefore, to ensure that they secure a sufficient return on the total assets at their disposal.

Liquidity
Current Ratio:

$$\frac{\text{Current Assets} \quad £340\,000}{\text{Current Liabilities} \quad £100\,000} = \underline{3.4}$$

Current assets are cash and items which, sooner or later, will be converted into cash. Current liabilities, on the other hand, represent a claim on the liquid resources of a business. Quite clearly, therefore, there must be the right relationship between current assets and current liabilities. When the current ratio is too low there is a danger that the business will not be able to pay its current commitments. When the current ratio is too high it is likely that too much cash is tied up in the current assets.

Acid Test Ratio:

$$\frac{\text{Liquid Assets} \quad £220\,000}{\text{Current Liabilities} \quad £100\,000} = \underline{2.2}$$

The acid test ratio is similar to, but more stringent than, the current ratio as a measure of liquidity. It relates to the current liabilities just cash and items which are capable of being converted into cash within a short period. The acid test ratio is, therefore, a strict and effective test of the short-term solvency of the business.

Rate of Stock Turnover:
Let us assume that the closing stock shown in the Balance Sheet is typical of the stock levels maintained by the company.

$$\frac{\text{Cost of Sales} \quad £1\,200\,000}{\text{Stock at Cost} \quad £120\,000} = \underline{10.0}$$

The rate of stock turnover measures the speed with which stocks are re-purchased, re-sold or turned over. In this particular case the average stock kept represents more than one month's operational requirements. The right, appropriate, rate of stock turnover can only be determined in relation to a particular type of business. Whatever the type of business operation, a downward trend in the rate of stock turnover will be an indication of over-buying, a tendency to keep excessive stocks. Conversely, an upward trend will show that comparatively lower stocks are being maintained in relation to the sales volume.

■ SELF ASSESSMENT QUESTIONS

1 The Alpha Company's balance sheets for its last two financial year ends are given below:

	31 May 1986		31 May 1987	
Fixed Assets	£	£	£	£
Plant and Equipment	1 620 000		1 980 000	
Accumulated Depreciation	600 000		780 000	
		1 020 000		1 200 000
Current Assets				
Cash	136 000		100 000	
Marketable Securities	180 000		150 000	
Debtors (net)	184 000		200 000	
Prepayments	40 000		50 000	
Inventory	240 000		300 000	
	780 000		800 000	
Current Liabilities	260 000		400 000	
Net Current Assets		520 000		400 000
Net Total Assets		1 540 000		1 600 000
Financed By:				
Long-term Loan	700 000		700 000	
Share Capital	250 000		250 000	
Share Premium	300 000		300 000	
Retained Earnings	290 000		350 000	
		1 540 000		1 600 000

Required:
Evaluate the financial position of the Alpha Company at 31 May, 1986, and at 31 May, 1987. Comment upon the changes between these dates.

(Institute of Marketing)

2 Explain what you understand by:
(a) accounting ratios;
(b) operating ratios;
(c) balance sheet ratios;
(d) profit and loss ratios.
3 Distinguish between profitability ratios and liquidity ratios; and give three examples of each.
4 A company operates a number of restaurants and, set out below, is some information relating to the Clacton Promenade Restaurant, in respect of six months ended 30 June 19...

	Jan	Feb	Mar	Apr	May	Jun
	£	£	£	£	£	£
Sales: Meals	20 000	22 000	23 000	27 000	32 000	45 000
Drinks	8 000	8 500	9 000	11 000	13 000	18 000
Total	28 000	30 500	32 000	38 000	45 000	63 000
No. of Guests	3 500	3 800	3 900	4 700	5 400	7 500
No. of Employees	26	26	27	27	32	36

You are required to calculate appropriate ratios and comment on:
(a) the structure and pattern of the restaurant's sales volume and
(b) the monthly size of the labour force. What advice would you offer to the company in relation to the second half-year?
5 The following are the accounts of a small limited company for the last two years:

Revenue Accounts for year ended 31 August

	1986		1987	
	£	£	£	£
Sales (all on credit)		100 000		120 000
Cost of Sales		60 000		80 000
Gross Profit		40 000		40 000
Administration Costs	8 000		8 500	
Distribution Costs	10 000	18 000	15 500	24 000
Net Profit		22 000		16 000

Balance Sheets as at 31 August

	1986		1987	
	£	£	£	£
Fixed Assets (Net)		74 000		90 000
Current Assets				
Stock	20 000		25 000	
Debtors	18 000		27 000	
Bank	3 000	41 000	—	52 000
Current Liabilities				
Creditors	18 000		25 000	
Overdraft	—		4 000	
		(18 000)		(29 000)
		97 000		113 000
Long-term Loans		17 000		17 000
		80 000		96 000
Financed by				
Ordinary Share Capital		50 000		50 000
Reserves		30 000		46 000
		80 000		96 000

(Ignore Tax and Dividends)

You are required to:
(a) State the Working Capital for both years.
(b) Calculate two Profitability Ratios for both years.
(c) Calculate two Liquidity Ratios for both years.
(d) Calculate the average number of days' credit extended to debtors for both years.
(e) Briefly comment on the performance of the company over the last two years.

(Institute of Commercial Management)

6 The following figures were extracted from the books of a small company:

	31 Jan	28 Feb	31 Mar
	£	£	£
Debtors	12 000	13 000	12 000
Creditors	14 000	16 000	19 000
Accrued Expenses	3 000	6 000	8 000
Cash	8 000	8 000	7 000
Stocks	20 000	24 000	26 000

You are required to:
(a) calculate the working capital, current ratio and acid test ratio at the end of each month;
(b) comment on the liquidity of the company.

9 | Planning finance

■ INTRODUCTION

Business organizations have a variety of objectives; and these will tend to vary somewhat from one case to another; also a given organization will see its objectives rather differently over a period of time. The principal objectives which a business may wish to achieve are:

    (a) profit maximization;
    (b) satisficing – where a 'satisfactory' rather than maximum profit is sought;
    (c) achieving a given rate of growth;
    (d) securing a given share of the market.

Business organizations will strive to achieve such objectives by obtaining funds from various sources and by various methods and investing such funds in appropriate assets such as: buildings, plant, machinery, stocks, etc. Both the choice of the right method of finance and the investment of such finance in the right assets are most critical to the achievement of the objectives of the business.

The availability and cost of finance will depend on a number of factors operating nationally, such as: changes in the level of bank credit; changes in the level of savings; movements of funds into and out of the country and, finally, government policy with regard to its own borrowing.

Additionally the availability and cost of finance will depend on the industry and company concerned. Businesses within a new and dynamic industry will find it easier to borrow than those in declining industries. Some industries/ business operations are regarded as more risky than others and will, therefore, find it relatively more difficult to raise finance. Smaller companies find it more difficult to borrow money and, invariably, pay a higher rate of interest than larger companies. Finally, lending institutions will always take a keen interest in the track record of the organization – as evidenced by its accounts for the last few years.

Basically, a business needs capital for two purposes: (a) capital to finance the acquisition of the fixed assets – premises, plant, equipment, etc. and (b) working capital which is needed – in the form of stocks of raw materials, finished goods, cash, etc. – to support its day-to-day operations. These two components of capital constitute the permanent capital of the business. Such permanent capital should be raised as long-term capital as, clearly, the premises, plant, stocks, etc. will be required over a long period of years.

In addition to its long-term permanent capital a business will require, from time to time, additional funds for medium-term and short-term purposes. Such additional capital, repayable within several years, should be raised as a medium- or short-term capital. It should be remembered, therefore, that when raising funds it is important to have in mind the appropriate time scale. Quite clearly, financing a long-term project by borrowing 'short' is, to say the least, imprudent.

■ SOURCES AND METHODS OF FINANCE

Once the financial requirements have been determined, it is necessary to select the right source and method of finance. 'Source of finance' relates to where the finance is obtained. 'Method of finance' relates to the manner in which such finance is obtained. Thus the investing public is a source of finance, and we may obtain funds from this source by using different methods, e.g. by the issue of ordinary shares or preference shares.

Finance may be obtained from two main sources: internal and external sources and these are now discussed below.

Internal sources

RETAINED PROFITS
Retained profits or 'plough back' are an important source of funds. A business which is profitable, will, therefore, be able to finance a high proportion of its capital projects from this internal source. Whilst we should regard retained profits as an important source of funds, we should remember that such funds are available at the expense of dividends. And, as it is important for a company to have funds for expansion and pay regular dividends, the right balance must be struck between these two claims on profits. Statistical information indicates that retained profits amount to some 40 per cent of the capital employed by British companies; and their importance should not be underestimated.

PROVISION FOR DEPRECIATION
As explained elsewhere, depreciation is a non-cash expense. Each year, therefore, we debit depreciation in the Profit and Loss Account, but there is no corresponding outflow of cash. Whilst, consequently, the provision for depreciation reduces the net profit, its net effect is to generate cash. In some businesses a high proportion of total capital is invested in depreciable assets such

as plant, equipment, machinery, etc. The provision for depreciation will, in such circumstances, constitute an important source of finance.

TAX PROVISION

Corporation tax is payable about a year after the profits have been earned. In normal circumstances there is an almost permanent provision for taxation in the accounts; and this means that the business enjoys the use of the moneys involved on one year's profits. This is tantamount to a permanent financing arrangement.

REDUCTION IN CURRENT ASSETS

In both manufacturing and trading organizations stock levels may be quite considerable in relation to the turnover of the enterprise. Also, where credit control is lax, debtors may rise to several weeks' credit sales. If, therefore, we can control both stock levels and debtors then we can make available additional cash for financing the business operation.

External sources

ORDINARY SHARES

The two important characteristics of ordinary shares are that they give the shareholders voting rights and that they entitle them to a periodic dividend, which varies with the amount of profits earned. Ordinary shares are normally issued to provide the bulk of the long-term, permanent finance required.

PREFERENCE SHARES

Preference shareholders do not normally enjoy voting rights, but are entitled to a fixed rate of dividend (e.g. 8%) irrespective of profits earned. Whilst ordinary shareholders' dividends depend on currently earned profits, preference shareholders can look, each year, to the same percentage of dividend. Preference shares may be redeemable (repayable) after a number of years or irredeemable. They are, however, generally regarded as a part of the permanent capital of the company.

RIGHTS ISSUE

This is a method of issuing shares to existing shareholders in proportion to their holdings. Thus a company's rights issue may be on the basis of 1:2, which means that shareholders would be offered one new share for every two shares already held by them. Rights issues have been popular in recent years; they are an inexpensive method of raising capital and are generally assured of success.

DEBENTURES

'Debenture' is simply the name given to the document which acknowledges a debt. The terms governing a debenture are normally controlled by a trust deed, which sets out the conditions of the contract between the company and the debentureholders. Debentureholders are normally entitled to a fixed rate of interest which has to be paid even when the company is trading at a loss. The security offered by the company may be of two kinds:

(a) a 'fixed charge' – on specific assets, e.g. freehold buildings of the company;

(b) a 'floating charge' – on all the assets owned by the company.

BANK OVERDRAFT

This is probably the most common and most flexible method of raising finance. Banks, however, see overdrafts as temporary arrangements, and they do not approve of customers who use overdrafts as permanent finance.

BANK LOANS

Unlike bank overdrafts – which are in theory repayable on demand – bank loans are repayable at a specified future date or by instalments over a specified period of time. Bank loans are normally quite small amounts in relation to the capital of a company. Also they are made for short periods.

HIRE PURCHASE

Hire purchase relates to the purchase of assets, e.g. motor cars, which have a relatively short life. Purchasers pay the initial deposit and, subsequently, regular, fixed amounts over a given period, at the end of which the goods become their property. Interest rates in hire purchase agreements tend to be quite high. There are, however, tax advantages – as full capital allowances may be claimed on the cash value of the asset acquired during the first year of the hire purchase agreement.

LEASING

This is a similar method to hire purchase which enables the company to acquire capital equipment out of income. Generally, lease finance is more expensive than short-term loans and bank overdrafts. Leasing agreements have been quite popular in recent years; and almost any item of equipment may be leased. Consequently leasing may be regarded as a method of short-, medium- or long-term finance.

SALE-AND-LEASE-BACK

This is a method of raising long-term finance, in which a business will sell its property to an insurance company or pension fund, and then lease it back for an agreed term – frequently 50 years or more. The advantage of this arrangement is that the business realizes the full value of its asset and is able to invest the proceeds more profitably. Sale-and-lease-back agreements have, however, some disadvantages. The seller (vendor) of the property loses the right to modify the property without the freeholder's consent and is committed to occupy the property for a long period of years. Also the cost of using the property may be quite high – especially where rent reviews are frequent.

FACTORING

Factoring is a method of raising finance under which a finance house will buy the invoiced debts, i.e. the debtors of a business. The result of this arrangement is that the business obtains immediate cash from its credit sales, although of course there is a charge for this service. Whilst some factoring firms are reluctant to accept responsibility for any bad debts, most will provide this service (known as 'del credere' insurance) and charge a commission based on the risks involved.

TRADE CREDITORS

A common form of short-term finance is the credit extended by suppliers. This is, of course, finance for which no charge is made. One should, however, be cautious, as failure to pay creditors promptly may result in loss of cash discounts and indeed suppliers' goodwill.

SPECIAL FINANCIAL ORGANIZATIONS

There are one or two special organizations financed essentially by banks. These provide funds to companies/organizations which, for some reason, find it difficult to borrow funds from existing, customary sources. The two, most important, of these are described below.

Industrial and Commercial Finance Corporation PLC (ICFC):
This institution provides finance to smaller and medium-sized companies. The loans are both medium- and long-term, for periods of up to twenty years.

Finance Corporation for Industry PLC (FCI):
This institution has similar functions to ICFC but makes loans which are considerably larger – certainly at least in excess of £1 million. Also, as in the case of the ICFC, the finance made available by the FCI is both medium- and long-term.

Capital gearing

The term 'capital gearing' relates to the respective proportions of debt capital (i.e. preference shares and loans) and equity capital (i.e. ordinary share capital). Where equity capital is small in relation to debt capital, the company is said to be 'highly geared'. Where, conversely, debt capital is small in relation to the ordinary shares capital, the capital gearing is low.

The advantage of high capital gearing is that, in times of good profitability, shareholders' rewards are particularly high. When profits are low, however, the payment of loan interest, etc. may absorb most of the profits, leaving almost nothing for ordinary shareholders. It is therefore essential to make sure that the capital gearing of a company is right. Let us take an example.

EXAMPLE

A company requires a capital of £400 000 and the capital may be arranged in two different ways as indicated below. Method 1 indicates high capital gearing and Method 2 low capital gearing. Let us assume that net profit in Year 1 is £40 000 and in Year 2 £25 000. The two alternative capital structures and subsequent distribution of profits are shown below.

(a) Capital Structure

	Method 1	Method 2
	£	£
Bank Loan – 8%	200 000	20 000
Preference Shares – 7½%	120 000	80 000
Ordinary Shares	80 000	300 000
Total	400 000	400 000

high gearing   *low gearing*   *O,K.* (handwritten annotations)

(b) Distribution of Profits – Year 1

	£	£
Bank Loan – 8%	16 000	1 600
Preference Shares – 7½%	9 000	6 000
Ordinary Shares	15 000	32 400
	40 000	40 000

40,000
9,000 (handwritten annotations)

(c) Distribution of Profits – Year 2

	£	£
Bank Loan – 8%	16 000	1 600
Preference Shares – 7½%	9 000	6 000
Ordinary Shares	—	17 400
	25 000	25 000

With high profits (£40 000) in Year 1, Method 1 gives the ordinary shareholders a very high dividend of 18.75% and Method 2, 10.8%. When, in Year 2, profits drop to £25 000, Method 1 results in no profits being available to ordinary shareholders; and Method 2 provides for a dividend of only 5.80%. Students will appreciate, therefore, that capital gearing is an important factor which should be taken into account when planning the capital structure of a company.

SELF ASSESSMENT QUESTIONS

1 Write short, explanatory notes on the following internal sources of capital:
(a) retained profits;
(b) provision for depreciation;
(c) tax provision;
(d) reduction of current assets.

2 Give a brief outline of the following external sources of capital:
(a) ordinary shares;
(b) preference shares;
(c) rights issues;
(d) debentures;
(e) bank overdrafts;
(f) bank loans;
(g) hire purchase;
(h) leasing,
(i) sale-and-lease-back;
(j) factoring;
(k) trade creditors.

3 A company wishes to raise additional funds to finance an expansion of its activities. The management seeks your advice in selecting between the two alternatives, i.e. whether to make a 'rights' issue to existing shareholders or to issue debentures.

Required:
(a) A comprehensive explanation of what is meant by each of the two above alternatives.
(b) A description of the effect of each proposal on the profits of the company.
(c) A recommendation of which alternative should be adopted assuming profits show a continuing upward trend.   (Association of Business Executives)

4 Distinguish clearly between 'sources' and 'methods' of finance.

5 Alpha Ltd and Omega Ltd have contrasting capital structures.

	Alpha Ltd £000	Omega Ltd £000
Ordinary Shares	1 200	300
Preference Shares (10%)	—	750
Debentures (10%)	300	450
	£1 500	£1 500

Discuss the relative gearing of the two companies, the cost of financing their non-equity shares and debentures and the possible fluctuations of profits available to ordinary shareholders.   (Association of Business Executives – Modified)

10 Assessment of capital projects

■ INTRODUCTION

The aim of this present chapter is to introduce students to the principal methods of assessing capital projects. These methods – although they are not normally used from one day to another – are important for several reasons.

Resources are always scarce and – whether as private individuals or business executives – we never have sufficient resources to purchase or do all the things we would like to. Thus a trading organization may have accumulated, say, £200 000, which is not currently required for any particular purpose. The question which then arises is: 'what shall we do with the £200 000?' On reflection it will be found that the cash may be spent/invested in a number of different ways. It may be desirable to acquire an additional selling outlet, modernize some of the existing stores, computerize all accounting procedures, invest the cash in stocks and shares, keep it in the bank on deposit, etc. The conclusion from this is that, whatever the resources at our disposal, they are never sufficient in relation to our aims, plans and ambitions. And this surely means that we have to ration resources and apply them in the most advantageous manner, having due regard to the principal objectives of the business/organization concerned.

The decisions which are referred to here involve large amounts of resources. Thus if the choice is between the construction of a new building to house the head office and the purchase of a department store in a big city, the sums involved are quite considerable. Also it should be noted that these decisions relate to a long period of time: once we have built the new head office premises we have to 'live' with the decision for a long period of years. It should be appreciated, therefore, that the longer the time for which resources are committed, the more essential it is to ensure that we use the right method in the decision-making process.

There are three principal methods of assessing capital projects: (a) pay-back, (b) return on investment and (c) discounted cash flow (DCF).

They don't consider infl.

◼ PAY-BACK

The essential concept of pay-back is simple: we relate the additional cash resulting from a project to the cost of the project and decide how long it will take to recover the latter from the former. Thus, if we spend £10 000 on a project and this results in an addition to our cash of £2 000 p.a., the pay-back period is five years. Other things being equal, where there are several projects being considered, we would choose the project with the shortest pay-back period. It should be noted that the <u>two essential elements</u> in the <u>concept of pay-back</u> are <u>cash</u> and <u>time.</u>

EXAMPLE

The head office of a national distribution company employs three clerks to process weekly reports from its depots. The work is currently done manually and the annual cost of this section of the accounts department is shown below.

	£	£
Salaries		
(a) 3 clerks @ £12 000 p.a.	36 000	
(b) Accounts Supervisor @ £12 000 p.a.	12 000	48 000
Other Costs:		
Stationery, etc.		2 000
Total		£50 000

It is now proposed to computerize this work and the cost of a suitable computer is £20 000. It is estimated that the effective life of the computer is five years. The annual cost of the computerized system is estimated as follows.

	£	£
Salaries:		
(a) Computer Operator @ £14 000 p.a.	14 000	
(b) Part-time Assistant @ £7 000 p.a.	7 000	
(c) Section Supervisor @ £16 000 p.a.	16 000	37 000
Other costs:		
(a) Depreciation	4 000	
(b) Stationery, Maintenance, etc.	3 000	7 000
Total		44 000

As <u>depreciation</u> is a <u>non-cash cost,</u> the cash outflow resulting from the new system is (£44 000 less £4 000) £40 000 per annum and the annual cash savings are £10 000 p.a. The pay-back period is therefore:

$$\frac{\text{Cost of computerized system} - £20\ 000}{\text{Annual cash savings} - £10\ 000} = \underline{2\ \text{years}}$$

The pay-back method has two main advantages. It is conceptually simple, easy to understand. Also it is easy to apply. The method has, unfortunately, some disadvantages. First, it is concerned with just the first few years: what happens after the pay-back period is not taken into account. Secondly, pay-back ignores the time-value of money and assumes that £1 in the future has the same value as £1 today. Finally, the method has an incorrect orientation. When we make business decisions, we should make them by reference to how they affect the objectives of the business concerned. In pay-back we are concerned with the recovery of the cost of a project and not its profitability. In conclusion it should be said that pay-back is a useful additional indicator in the process of decision making. On its own it is not an adequate criterion for business decisions.

■ RETURN ON INVESTMENT

In this method we are interested in the relationship between the capital cost of a project and the resulting net profit. The formula for calculating the return on investment is:

$$\frac{\text{Average net profit}}{\text{Average cost of project}} \times 100 = \text{Return on Investment}$$

Average net profit is, quite simply, the average net profit for a given number of years. The term 'average cost of project', however, requires some explanation. When we invest in plant, machinery, etc., the original sum invested is reduced each year by the depreciation written off to the Profit and Loss Account. If, for example, we purchase a computer for £20 000 with an effective life of four years then (using the straight-line method of depreciation) we, so to speak, recover £5 000 a year by debiting that amount in the Profit and Loss Account. The amount invested in the computer is £15 000 at the end of the first year, £10 000 at the end of the second year, etc. and finally, at the end of the fourth year, it is nil. In this particular case the average cost of the project is £10 000. For the purpose of the return on investment method we take the initial cost of the project and divide it by two to arrive at its average cost.

EXAMPLE

Two alternative projects, A and B, are being considered by a company. They have an identical initial cost of £800 000 each. The return on investment for the two projects would be calculated as shown below. Let us assume that each project has an effective life of six years and that annual profits are as shown below.

	A	**B**
Average cost of project	£400 000	£400 000
Resulting Profits:	£	£
Year 1	220 000	50 000
Year 2	150 000	50 000
Year 3	90 000	80 000
Year 4	80 000	100 000
Year 5	40 000	160 000
Year 6	20 000	180 000
	600 000	620 000
Average Net Profit	£100 000	£103 333
Return on Investment	25.0%	25.8%

The main advantage of the return on investment method is that it is easy to understand and apply. Also it has the right orientation: it is concerned with profitability, which is always seen as a major business objective. Its only major disadvantage is that it ignores the time-value of money. In our example, for instance, it is assumed that £1 of net profit in Year 6 has the same value as £1 of net profit in Year 1. This, of course, is not true; and although Project B appears more profitable most of the profits are generated here towards the end of the life of the project, when every £1 has a lower value than at the beginning of the project. This is explained further in the section on discounted cash flow which now follows.

■ DISCOUNTED CASH FLOW (DCF)

We mentioned earlier in this chapter the importance of the time element in relation to the value of money. The problem of the time-value may be explained as follows: £1.00 now is worth more than £1.00 in, say, a year's time, because if invested now at, say, 10% it will increase in value to £1.10. Similarly £1.00 now is equivalent (assuming compound interest at 10%) to £1.21 in two years' time.

We may express this compounding process as shown below.

£1.00 will accumulate to:
  (a) $£1.00 (1 + r)$ .... in one year's time.
  (b) $£1.00 (1 + r)^2$ .... in two years' time.
  (c) $£1.00 (1 + r)^3$ .... in three years' time.
Where r denotes the relevant rate of interest.

We may now calculate the present value of £1.00 at some point in time in the future, as follows:

£1.00 receivable in n years' time is now worth:

$$\frac{£1.00}{(1 + r)^n}$$

Consequently:

(a) £1.00 receivable in one year's time is worth $\dfrac{£1.00}{(1.10)} = £0.909$

(b) £1.00 receivable in two years' time is worth $\dfrac{£1.00}{(1.10)^2} = £0.826$

(c) £1.00 receivable in three years' time is worth $\dfrac{£1.00}{(1.10)^3} = £0.751$

The process of finding the present day value of money receivable (or indeed payable) in the future is known as discounting. In DCF calculations we would not resort to the use of a formula as in the above examples. Instead we would consult DCF tables where the conversion factors are given for different rates of interest and periods of time.

If we refer to the Appendix on p. 161, we will see the conversion factors for 1–15 years and a variety of interest rates. Thus the conversion factor for 5 years and 10% is 0.621. This means that £1 000 receivable or payable in 5 years' time has a present-day value of £621. The conversion factor for 3 years and 8% is 0.794 which, again, means that £1 000 receivable or payable in three years' time has a present-day value of £794. As already explained, it also means that £794 invested at 8% over three years will produce – at compound interest – £1 000.

EXAMPLE

Jack lends Jill £1 000. She promises, and repays, the loan at the rate of £250 a year over four years. The value of the money repaid by Jill is, assuming interest at 10%, worth as follows:

Year	Amount Repaid £	Conversion Factor	Present Value £
1	250.00	0.909	227.25
2	250.00	0.826	206.50
3	250.00	0.751	187.75
4	250.00	0.683	170.75
	1 000.00		792.25

From the above calculation it may be seen that the present-day value of the money repaid by Jill is £792.25. Jack's loss (and Jill's profit) on the transaction is £207.75.

Students will appreciate from this first example, that conversion factors are a means of expressing future cash flows – at various points in time and at various rates of interest – in terms of their present-day values. The cash flows which are the subject of DCF problems are flows of cash and should not be confused with flows of net profit. 'Cash inflow', or positive cash flow, is cash received; 'cash outflow', or negative cash flow, is cash paid out; finally the difference between these two flows is described as 'net cash flow'.

The technique of DCF may be applied in two different ways, known as the NPV (Net Present Value) method and the IRR (Internal Rate of Return) method.

■ THE NPV METHOD

The net present value method is applied as follows. We assume a particular rate of interest and discount all future cash flows to arrive at their present-day values. The excess of the discounted total over the cost of the project is known as the net present value. Quite clearly, the higher the net present value the more attractive the project.

EXAMPLE

A company is considering two projects, involving a capital cost of £400 000 each. The life of each project is six years and the net cash flows are as shown below. Assume that the appropriate rate of interest is 10 per cent.

Year	Conversion Factor	Project A Net Cash Flow £	Project A Present Value £	Project B Net Cash Flow £	Project B Present Value £
1	0.909	210 000	190 890	50 000	45 450
2	0.826	160 000	132 160	60 000	49 560
3	0.751	90 000	67 590	80 000	60 080
4	0.683	80 000	54 640	100 000	68 300
5	0.621	40 000	24 840	160 000	99 360
6	0.564	20 000	11 280	180 000	101 520
		600 000	481 400	630 000	424 270
less Cost of Project			400 000		400 000
Net Present Value			81 400		24 270

It should be pointed out that Project B will generate a higher net cash flow than Project A. The latter has, however, a more favourable net cash flow profile (i.e. most of the net cash flow materializes at the beginning of the life of the project). In consequence Project A is preferable to Project B. Finally, it should be noted that in both cases we have a positive net present value – both projects are profitable. Where the net present value is negative there is no case for going ahead with the project as a loss would be incurred.

■ THE IRR METHOD

The procedure in the case of the internal rate of return method is as follows. We discount future net cash flows at various rates of interest, until the discounted total (of net cash flows) is equal to the cost of the project. The rate of interest which is instrumental in securing this equality is known as the internal rate of return.

EXAMPLE

A company is considering a project costing £962,800 and having an effective life of six years. The net cash flows will be as shown below. You are required to find the internal rate of return for the project. Students should realize that the only course of action possible here is to proceed by trial and error. Let us, therefore, try 8 per cent.

Year	Net Cash Flow £	Conversion Factor	Present Value £
1	420 000	0.926	388 920
2	320 000	0.857	274 240
3	180 000	0.794	142 920
4	160 000	0.735	117 600
5	80 000	0.681	54 480
6	40 000	0.630	25 200
	1 200 000		1 003 360

962,800
1,003,360

The discounted total of £1 003 360, is considerably more than the cost of the project; and it is clear, therefore, that we have not used a sufficiently high rate of interest. Let us, therefore, try 12 per cent.

Year	Net Cash Flow £	Conversion Factor	Present Value £
1	420 000	0.893	375 060
2	320 000	0.797	255 040
3	180 000	0.712	128 160
4	160 000	0.636	101 760
5	80 000	0.567	45 360
6	40 000	0.507	20 280
	1 200 000		925 660

925 660

Evidently our second attempt, using 12 per cent, has not been successful as, this time, the discounted total is below the cost of the project. Let us, therefore, try 10 per cent.

Year	Net Cash Flow £	Conversion Factor	Present Value £
1	420 000	0.909	381 780
2	320 000	0.826	264 320
3	180 000	0.751	135 180
4	160 000	0.683	109 280
5	80 000	0.621	49 680
6	40 000	0.564	22 560
	1 200 000		962 800

The discounted total is now equal to the cost of the project; and the internal rate of return is 10 per cent.

Let us now comment on the significance of the net present value and the internal rate of return. The net present value of £81 400 in the previous example is the profit on the project. If the £400 000 required for the project was borrowed at 10 per cent then the £81 400 is the net gain after repayment of the loan and interest on the reducing balance. The internal rate of return in the case of the second example is 10 per cent. Had we borrowed the money for the project, £962 800, at 10 per cent the gain on the project would have been nil. If, on the other hand, the project was financed by a loan at, say, 7 per cent, the gain would then be 3 per cent. Where, therefore, the internal rate of return is in excess of the cost of capital the project appears to be worth while.

Some additional explanations

As already explained DCF is concerned with flows of cash and not the accounting concept of profit. Consequently depreciation should not be taken into account in DCF calculations: it does not entail a cash outflow.

Net cash flow will always be affected by the payment of tax liabilities. It is essential to calculate accurately both the amount of tax and the timing of the payment to ensure correct figures of cash outflow.

Whenever we use the net present value method we must have a rate of interest at which to discount the future cash flows. The choice of the rate of interest must always reflect the cost of capital to the business. Thus when we borrow finance for a project at 10 per cent, we must discount future cash flows at 10 per cent. When a project is financed with internal funds – which is often the case – it is essential to calculate the cost of capital to the company, having regard to all the sources of capital: ordinary shares, preference shares, debentures, etc. If a company has a debt/equity ratio of 2:3 (say ordinary share capital of £300 000 and debentures to the value of £200 000) and the ordinary shareholders required a return of 15 per cent and the debentures were issued at 8 per cent, then the cost of capital will be:

Debt – £200 000 @ 8% = £16 000
Equity – £300 000 @ 15% = 45 000
£500 000 £61 000

The cost of capital will, therefore, be:

$$\frac{61}{500} \times 100 = 12.2\%$$

and this will then be the rate of interest used for DCF purposes.

PRACTICE PROBLEM

Your company is about to launch a new product. This will require the abandonment of an existing line. You have been given the following information to assist you in selecting the products to abandon.

Product	Net sales income					
	year 1	year 2	year 3	year 4	year 5	year 6
A	£140 000	£40 000	£50 000	£60 000	£80 000	£100 000
B	80 000	80 000	80 000	80 000	80 000	
C	40 000	80 000	120 000	160 000		
New Line	30 000	80 000	105 000	320 000	354 000	400 000

The cost of capital is to be taken as 10%. The present value of £1 received in the future is:

year	1	2	3	4	5	6
	£.909	.826	.751	.683	.621	.564

You are required to:
(a) Calculate the present value of the future cash flows for the four products. State, giving your reasons, which product you would discontinue.
(b) State the advantages of the discounted cash flow method of investment appraisal.
(c) Compare this technique with the pay-back method.
(d) What other information would you, as a Marketing Manager, require before you make a final decision?

(Institute of Marketing)

SOLUTION

Part (a)

In order to decide which product should be discontinued, it is necessary to discount all future cash flows to arrive at their present values. The necessary calculations are shown below.

Year	Conv. Fact.	Product A NCF	Product A PV	Product B NCF	Product B PV	Product C NCF	Product C PV	New line NCF	New line PV
		£000	£000	£000	£000	£000	£000	£000	£000
1	.909	140	127 260	80	72 720	40	36 360	30	27 270
2	.826	40	33 040	80	66 080	80	66 080	80	66 080
3	.751	50	37 550	80	60 080	120	90 120	105	78 855
4	.683	60	40 980	80	54 640	160	109 280	320	218 560
5	.621	80	49 680	80	49 680			354	219 834
6	.564	100	56 400					400	225 600
			344 910		303 200		301 840		836 199

Product C has the lowest present value and, other things being equal, it is this product that should be discontinued.

Part (b)

The main advantage of DCF is that it takes into account the time-value of money. By means of appropriate conversion factors we can convert all future cash flows into their present-day equivalents. Irrespective of when such movements of cash take place we have a common denominator (present value) which is of immense value in decision making.

Part (c)

DCF is superior to pay-back in several respects. It looks at the whole life of the project, whilst pay-back is concerned with only the first few years, known as the pay-back period. It is a better oriented method, concerned with the creation of wealth, whilst pay-back looks at the recovery of the cost of the project. Finally, DCF recognizes the time-value of money, whilst the pay-back method implies that cash in the future has the same value as cash now. The one thing the two methods have in common is that they both look at movements of cash rather than net profit.

Part (d)

The final decision on which product should be dropped would not be made solely by reference to the present values of the three products – particularly as the difference between Product B and Product C is marginal. Some of the other important considerations might be:
(i)   If Product C is a prestige product its continuance might be desirable in terms of public relations and the image of the company.
(ii) The skills involved in the manufacture of Product C may be useful/relevant to the

manufacture of other existing products or the possible introduction of new lines in the future.

(iii) The manufacture of Product C may involve the use of expensive, highly specialized plant and machinery. If Product C were to be discontinued the plant and machinery might be difficult to sell and would have to be written off.

■ SELF ASSESSMENT QUESTIONS

1 Write short explanatory notes on each of the following:
(a) pay-back;
(b) return on investment;
(c) discounted cash flow.

2 Compare and contrast the net present value method and the internal rate of return method.

3 There are broadly three ways of appraising capital investment:
● Rate of Return on Investment
● Pay-back Method
● DCF
(a) Detail the advantages and disadvantages of each.
(b) Explain the circumstances in which you would consider each one the most appropriate.

(Association of Business Executives)

4 Your company is considering an investment of £50 000 in a franchise operation. The potential product life is estimated at five years and the investment value is assumed to be nil at the end of that period. Anticipated cash flows after paying all running expenses are:

Year 1	£15 000	Year 4	£25 000
Year 2	£20 000	Year 5	£10 000
Year 3	£25 000		

The company's cost of capital is 20%.
Required:
(a) An evaluation of the proposal using:
  (i)   Pay-back
  (ii) Net Present Value
  (iii) Internal Rate of Return
(b) Briefly explain the significance of each of the above appraisal methods.

(Association of Business Executives)

5 Your company is contemplating replacement of one of its machines. Two alternative ways of purchase have been examined:
● outright purchase, and
● credit purchase over five years.

The machine will cost £100 000 if purchased for cash, or £20 000 deposit followed by five equal annual instalments of £20 000 each, if purchased on credit terms. It is estimated that repairs will cost £5 000 and £10 000 during years 2 and 4 respectively and that the scrap value will be £10 000 at the end of year 5. Your company's cost of capital is 10% per annum.

Which purchase method would you advise and why?

Describe the following methods of investment appraisal:
(a) Accounting rate of return;
(b) Pay-back method.
Present value of £1 at 10% cost of capital received at the end of year

1	.909
2	.826
3	.751
4	.683
5	.621

(Institute of Marketing)

6 The management of Chi Ltd has before it three mutually exclusive investment projects. Each project will require an initial investment of £50 000 and will have no residual value.

It is expected that the revenue less the outlays, receivable at the end of each year, will be as follows:
Project X £35 000 p a for 2 years.
Project Y £20 000 p a for 5 years.
Project Z £12 000 p a for 10 years.
The cost of capital to Chi Ltd is 15%.
(a) Calculate for each of the three projects:
(i) the pay-back period;
(ii) the accounting return (based on the initial investment);
(iii) the net present value (to the nearest £1): and rank the projects under each method.
(b) Advise management which of the projects should be accepted.

The present value of £1		*The present value of £1 per annum*	
Years	15%	Years	15%
1	0.869565	1	0.86956
2	0.756144	2	1.62571
3	0.657516	3	2.28323
4	0.571753	4	2.85498
5	0.497177	5	3.35216
6	0.432328	6	3.78448
7	0.375937	7	4.16042
8	0.326902	8	4.48732
9	0.284262	9	4.77158
10	0.247185	10	5.01877

(Institute of Marketing)

7 You work in the management accounts section of a company which has to decide which of two projects it will invest in. The following are the relevant data:

Project	X	Y
Initial Investment	£300 000	£300 000
Net surplus returns	£	£
Year 1	100 000	80 000
2	120 000	100 000
3	100 000	100 000
4	60 000	100 000
5	40 000	40 000

You are required to:
(a) State three major methods used for investment appraisal.
(b) Use the above data to demonstrate the three methods you have stated in (a).
(c) Which project would you recommend and why?

Use the following discount factors where you think it appropriate:

	10%
Year 0	1.000
1	0.909
2	0.826
3	0.752
4	0.683
5	0.621

(Institute of Commercial Management)

8 The directors of Kwikgro Fertilizer Ltd propose to buy a replacement item of processing plant costing £50 000. They estimate it will last ten years but would require a major overhaul, costing £20 000, at the end of the sixth year. The residual value at the end of ten years is assumed to be nil.

Savings in operator cost will result, reducing from £10 000 per year to £4 000 per year. Output, which can all be sold, can be increased by 2 000 tonnes per year due to improved plant capacity. Sales price is £40 per tonne and the variable cost of manufacture is £24 per tonne.

Required:
(a) A calculation of the annual cash flows resulting from the use of the new item of processing plant.
(b) A calculation of the net present value if the company requires a 20% rate of return.
(c) A calculation of the pay-back period of the investment.

(Association of Business Executives)

11 Managing working capital

■ INTRODUCTION

Every business enterprise requires two kinds of capital: fixed capital and working capital. Fixed capital is that part of total capital which is invested in land, buildings, plant and machinery, office equipment, etc. Working capital, on the other hand, is that part of total capital which supports the actual day-to-day operations: purchase of raw materials/finished goods, payment of current expenses such as wages, salaries, rents, rates, insurances, etc. It should be appreciated that a business may have ample premises, modern plant and equipment, a good product and satisfied customers and yet fail – if it does not have at its disposal adequate working capital.

The amount of working capital required by a business flows directly from the nature of the operation concerned. Thus business organizations such as manufacturing companies will necessarily require substantial stocks of raw materials and maintain adequate stocks of work-in-progress and finished goods. Similarly trading organizations, wholesalers, retailers, mail order houses, etc. will, of necessity, keep stocks frequently amounting to several hundred thousand pounds and constituting a large proportion of total capital.

On the other hand service industries – because they sell services rather than tangible, physical products – require a modest amount of working capital. Thus hotels, travel agents, firms of accountants, solicitors, management consultants and similar organizations will all manage with a relatively low amount of working capital and, frequently, a current ratio of just in excess of 1:1.

■ CONTROL OF WORKING CAPITAL

Where working capital constitutes a significant percentage of total capital, it is essential to institute regular and strict controls to ensure that all the liquid resources of the business are used efficiently. What is required, therefore, is a frequent check on: (a) total working capital and (b) the components of working capital.

Total working capital is normally controlled by means of a Monthly Statement of Working Capital illustrated below. The statement is simple in construction but typical of the kinds of statements of working capital used by most companies. In our example we show the position at the end of each quarter but, of course, month-end figures may be shown instead. An important advantage of the statement is that it shows clearly the trend in the two principal ratios – the current ratio and the acid test ratio.

Statement of Working Capital

	31 Dec. 19..		31 Mar. 19..		30 Jun. 19..	
	£	£	£	£	£	£
Current Assets:						
Cash at Bank	39 400		32 800		27 400	
Debtors	9 000		9 600		10 000	
Finished Goods	16 000		16 200		15 400	
Raw Materials	20 000	84 400	20 300	78 900	20 200	73 000
Current Liabilities:						
Creditors	30 800		34 100		38 000	
Accrued Expenses	5 000	35 800	6 200	40 300	6 000	44 000
Working Capital		48 600		38 600		29 000
Current Ratio		2.36		1.96		1.66
Acid Test Ratio		1.35		1.05		0.85

■ COMPONENTS OF WORKING CAPITAL

Let us now look at the individual components of working capital and examine the typical controls which are applied in each case.

Cash

The most important tool for controlling the cash position is the cash budget. As explained in Chapter 6, the cash budget will project, over a period of twelve months, all the cash inflows and outflows; and show the cash balance at the end of each month. In addition to this principal control measure, it is essential to review the cash position on at least a weekly basis. Cash is not only a valuable asset, but also the most liquid asset without which the smooth running of a business is impossible. In order to explain retrospective changes in cash position we prepare cash flow statements and these are explained later in the chapter.

Debtors

In businesses which sell on credit – and almost all do – debtors, if not controlled properly, may tie up a great deal of cash. Where debt collection is slack, bad debts may amount to a significant percentage of total credit sales. It cannot, therefore, be emphasized too strongly that credit control and debt collection must be regarded as very important elements in the control of a business operation. Most medium and all large businesses prepare a Monthly Statement of Debtors as illustrated below.

Monthly Statement of Debtors
as at 30 June 19..

	Date Incurred	Amount	Total
		£	£
Current Debts – due less than 1 month		145 476	145 476
Debts due more than 1 month:			
A C Kelly & Sons	May 4	24 350	
B K Williams Ltd	May 17	17 030	
M P Shilling & Co.	May 14	18 475	
Acton Trades Ltd	May 12	55 301	
S M Jones & Co.	May 19	42 906	158 062
Debts due more than 2 months:			
J G Lane & Co. Ltd	Apr 12	17 995	
B S Mulligan & Sons	Apr 2	4 771	
A K Cayman	Apr 22	20 345	43 111
Debts due more than 3 months:			
V Tardy & Co. Ltd	Mar 15	11 467	
N O Cash & Co.	Mar 4	25 443	36 910
TOTAL DEBTS			383 559

Stocks

As already mentioned the control of stock levels is of paramount importance. This necessitates an efficient system of stores control – including stock records, stores requisitions, etc. As suggested in Chapter 8 rates of stock turnover should be calculated at regular intervals to ensure that stock levels are correct in relation to the scale of operations. A company operating a number of retail outlets selling domestic appliances might have a monthly report prepared as shown below.

Domestic Appliances PLC
Monthly Report on Stock Levels – August 19..

Branch	Cost of Sales	Stock at Cost	Monthly RST	
			This Month	Last Month
Acton	45 000	18 000	2.5	2.6
Brent	32 000	14 000	2.3	2.4
Chiswick	84 000	65 000	1.3	1.2
Denham	127 000	47 000	2.7	2.5
Ealing	67 000	28 000	2.4	2.6

From the above report it appears that all branches operate at monthly rates of stock turnover of 2.3 – 2.6 with the exception of one (Chiswick); and the reasons for exceptionally high stock levels at this branch would have to be investigated.

Creditors

Almost all creditors supply goods/raw materials on credit and, additionally, offer cash discounts for prompt payment. Suppliers' credit is an important source of funds (see Chapter 9) – particularly in the case of new companies with limited resources. Also it should be appreciated that cash discounts – though normally shown in the Profit and Loss Account as 'Discounts Received' – have a direct and important bearing on the cost of sales and hence on gross profit margins. Finally it is important to control the creditors not only to ensure that all possible cash discounts are taken advantage of but also to retain the suppliers' goodwill through prompt payment of their accounts.

■ EFFECT OF TRANSACTIONS ON WORKING CAPITAL

In order to explain the effect of transactions on the working capital, it is first necessary to consider the basic structure of the balance sheet. Given below is a summarized balance sheet of XYZ Ltd.

XYZ Ltd
Balance Sheet as at ....

Share Capital	XXX		Fixed Assets	XXX
Debentures	XXX			
Current Liabilities	XXX		Current Assets	XXX
	XXX			XXX

We have drawn a double horizontal line, dividing all the balance sheet items into: (a) current items (which determine working capital), and (b) non-current items whose existence has no direct bearing on working capital. The imaginary horizontal line (it is not drawn on balance sheets) is a useful instrument in enabling us to classify transactions according to the effect they have on working capital.

Every business transaction has two aspects and requires a debit in one account and a credit in another. Some transactions will involve only accounts above the imaginary line and will not have any effect on working capital. Thus, when we write off depreciation we: (a) decrease the fixed asset and (b) decrease net profit. Both accounts are above the line and working capital is not affected. Some transactions operate on both sides of the horizontal line. For instance if we issue debentures, we have: (a) an increase in long-term liabilities (above the line) and (b) an increase in current assets (Cash at Bank, below the line). As there is no change in current liabilities, the effect is to increase working capital. Other transactions operate wholly below the line, and these have no effect on working capital. Let us now look at two examples. When we pay suppliers, we have: (a) a decrease in cash and (b) the same decrease in creditors. Working capital will, therefore, remain constant. When we buy stock, we have: (a) an increase in stock and (b) a decrease of the same magnitude in cash – with no effect on working capital. We may, therefore, divide business transactions into three categories, those which: (a) increase working capital; (b) decrease working capital, and (c) have no effect on working capital. With this in mind, let us consider the effect of several transactions on both working capital and cash in the example which now follows.

EXAMPLE

Set out below is a list of transactions of Domestic Appliances PLC. Show the effect of each transaction on: (a) the working capital of the company and (b) its cash position.

Transaction	Working Capital	Cash
Purchased Machinery for Cash: Explanation – (a) increase in fixed assets (above the line); (b) decrease in current assets (below the line).	Decrease	Decrease
Issued 8% Debentures: Explanation – (a) increase in long-term liabilities (above the line); (b) increase in current assets, i.e. cash (below the line).	Increase	Increase
Purchased Goods on Credit: Explanation – (a) increase in current assets (below the line); (b) increase in current liabilities (below the line).	None	None

Paid Creditors: Explanation – (a) decrease in current assets (below the line); (b) decrease in current liabilities (below the line).	None	Decrease
Depreciated Plant and Machinery: Explanation – (a) decrease in fixed assets (above the line); (b) decrease in net profit (above the line).	None	None
Collected Debts from Customers: Explanation – (a) increase in current assets (below the line); (b) decrease in current assets (below the line).	None	Increase
Repaid Long-term Loan: Explanation – (a) decrease in long-term liabilities (above the line); (b) decrease in current liabilities (below the line).	Decrease	Decrease

■ FUNDS FLOW STATEMENTS

The aims of a funds flow statement is to explain any change in the working capital of a business from one balance sheet date to another. It is important to remember that 'funds' for this purpose means working capital – i.e. current assets less current liabilities.

The usual procedure in the preparation of a funds flow statement is to ascertain the opening working capital, add sources of funds, deduct uses or applications of funds and, in this way, arrive at the closing amount of working capital.

Students should remember that all transactions, as explained, have one of three possible effects on working capital. Those which increase working capital we describe as 'sources of funds'; those which decrease working capital we describe as 'uses of funds' or 'applications of funds'; and finally there are those transactions which have no effect on working capital and these are of no direct interest in the context of funds flow statements.

The preparation of funds flow statements requires an understanding of the effect of profitable (and unprofitable) transactions on working capital. If, in a department store, we sell for cash goods which cost £100 for £150, the effect is as follows. We have a decrease in stock of £100; increase in cash of £150 – i.e. a net increase in current assets of £50. Also we have an increase of £50 in net profit – above the line. The effect of this profitable transaction is to increase working capital.

For the purposes of funds flow statements, therefore, net profit should be regarded as a source of funds; net loss should, conversely, be regarded as an application of funds. Finally net profit is arrived at after debiting depreciation in the Profit and Loss Account. As depreciation is a non-cash expense, it should be added back to net profit to arrive at the funds generated by operations.

EXAMPLE

Given below are the comparative balance sheets of the Brookmount Leisure Centre.

Comparative Balance Sheets

	£000	£000	£000	£000	£000
		1988		1989	Increase (Decrease)
Cash		400		360	(40)
Debtors		500		480	(20)
Prepayments		20		40	20
Stock		100		60	(40)
Fixed Assets	800		1 040		
less Aggregate Depreciation	200	600	240	800	200
Total		1 620		1 740	120
Creditors		300		100	(200)
Accrued Expenses		40		20	(20)
Profit & Loss A/c		80		120	40
Ordinary Shares		1 200		1 500	300
		1 620		1 740	120

The opening and closing amounts of working capital may be calculated as follows:

	1988	1989
	£000	£000
Cash	400	360
Debtors	500	480
Prepayments	20	40
Stock	100	60
	1 020	940
Creditors	300	100
Accrued Expenses	40	20
	340	120
Hence, Working Capital	680	820

The funds flow statement would be drawn up as follows:

Funds Flow Statement

	£000	£000
Opening Working Capital		680
add Sources of funds:		
Increase in Profit and Loss Account	40	
Depreciation	40	
Increase in Share Capital	300	380
		1 060
less Applications of funds:		
Increase in Fixed Assets	240	240
Closing Working Capital		820

■ CASH FLOW STATEMENTS

Many organizations prepare, in addition to funds flow statements, cash flow statements. Whilst the aim of the funds flow statement is to explain changes in working capital from one balance sheet date to another, the aim of the cash flow statement is to explain changes in the cash position, again, from one balance sheet to another.

The procedure in the preparation of cash flow statements is as follows. In order to explain the change in the cash position over a period of time (normally one year) we have to take into account not only the sources and applications of working capital, but also changes in individual current assets and current liabilities.

When we buy goods for cash, we have an increase in stocks and a corresponding decrease in cash. When, however, we buy goods on credit we conserve the cash resources. An increase in creditors, therefore, operates to increase the cash balance. When we collect cash from debtors, we increase our cash balance. Thus any increase in current liabilities represents a source of cash; any decrease in current liabilities is an application of cash. On the other hand, an increase in current assets represents an application of cash, whilst a decrease in current assets is a source of cash. With these basic principles in mind, we may now convert the funds flow statement of the Brookmount Leisure Centre into a cash flow statement.

Cash Flow Statement

	£000	£000
Opening Cash Balance		400
add Sources:		
Increase in Profit and Loss Account	40	
Depreciation	40	
Increase in Share Capital	300	
Decrease in Stock	40	
Decrease in Debtors	20	440
		840
less Applications:		
Increase in Fixed Assets	240	
Increase in Prepayments	20	
Decrease in Creditors	200	
Decrease in Accrued Expenses	20	480
Closing Cash Balance		360

■ SELF ASSESSMENT QUESTIONS

1 Distinguish between fixed capital and working capital.

2 Explain how a medium-sized trading organization would control its:

(a) cash;　　　　(c) stock;

(b) debtors;　　　(d) creditors.

3 From the figures given below prepare a statement of working capital.

	31.1.19..	28.2.19..	31.3.19..
	£	£	£
Cash at Bank	80 200	84 700	88 300
Raw Materials	37 500	42 300	31 300
Creditors	60 600	54 700	49 000
Debtors	21 600	29 400	32 900
Finished Goods	28 600	31 900	30 400
Accrued Expenses	12 000	17 000	17 600

4 Explain the effect of each of the following transactions on cash and working capital.

(a) Issue of shares – £500 000;

(b) Purchase for cash of machinery – £150 000;

(c) Payment of creditors – £30 000;
(d) Receipts from debtors – £50 000;
(e) Depreciation of fixed assets – £75 000;
(f) Sale for cash of fixed assets – £10 000;
(g) Purchase of goods on credit – £50 000;
(h) Sale of goods on credit – £110 000.

5 Using a working capital definition of funds, state (with reasons) whether or not each of the following transactions will affect an enterprise's flow of funds during a given period:
(a) declaration of a dividend;
(b) purchase of a warehouse;
(c) increase in finished goods inventory.

(Institute of Marketing – Modified)

6 From the comparative balance sheets given below prepare a funds flow statement and a cash flow statement.

Comparative Balance Sheets

	Year 1		Year 2		+Increase −Decrease
	£	£	£	£	£
Cash		20 000		10 000	−10 000
Debtors		2 000		4 000	+ 2 000
Stocks		6 000		4 000	− 2 000
Furniture	20 000		30 000		
Aggregate Depreciation	8 000	12 000	12 000	18 000	+ 6 000
Plant and Equipment	40 000		48 000		
Aggregate Depreciation	10 000	30 000	12 000	36 000	+ 6 000
Land and Buildings		80 000		100 000	+20 000
		150 000		172 000	+22 000
Creditors		10 000		8 000	− 2 000
Accrued Expenses		4 000		2 000	− 2 000
Profit and Loss Account		20 000		26 000	+ 6 000
Debentures		40 000		30 000	−10 000
Ordinary Shares		76 000		106 000	+30 000
		150 000		172 000	+22 000

(Schiller International University)

7 James Johnstone has the following balance sheets for the two most recent year ends:

	Year to 31.3.1985	Year to 31.3.1986
Capital	12 000	10 500
Long Term Loan	8 000	10 000
	£20 000	£20 500
Represented by:		
Fixtures	2 000	1 500
Plant	12 000	14 000
Inventory	8 000	9 000
Debtors	5 000	7 000
Cash	3 000	—
	£30 000	£31 500
Creditors	9 000	7 000
Accruals	1 000	2 000
Bank Overdraft	—	2 000
	10 000	11 000
	£20 000	£20 500

The following details are also available:

Plant Account

Balance at 31.3.1985	£12 000
Acquisitions during year	4 000
	16 000
Depreciation during year	2 000
Balance at 31.3.1986	14 000

Fixtures Account
Depreciation of £500 has been written off during the year.

Capital Account

Balance at 31.3.1985	£12 000
Net profit for year	4 000
New capital introduced	1 000
	17 000
Drawings	6 500
Balance at 31.3.1986	10 000

Required
(a) A funds flow statement for the business for the year to 31.3.1986 set out in an informative style.
(b) A commentary on the position that the funds flow statement reveals.

(Institute of Marketing)

12 Profit sensitivity analysis

■ INTRODUCTION

Profit sensitivity analysis (PSA) is a relatively new technique. It is easy to understand, but its main advantage is that: (a) it gives us a greater insight into how a business makes its profits; (b) enables us to identify the orientation of the business (i.e. shows whether the business is cost oriented or market oriented) and, finally, (c) indicates the correct approach to cost control on the one hand and revenue control on the other.

The application of PSA resolves itself into three relatively easy steps, as explained below.

(a) First we must identify the key factors which operate to influence net profit. These should be determined primarily by reference to the Profit and Loss Account. Typically, in a manufacturing company we will have on the cost side: (a) direct materials; (b) direct labour; (c) direct expenses; (d) production overhead; (e) administration overheads; and (f) selling and distribution overheads. On the revenue side we will have the sales volume (or the number of units) and the price level.

(b) Secondly we have to calculate in respect of each key factor a *profit multiplier*, which measures the effect on net profit of a change (increase or decrease) in that key factor. To do this we assume a small (usually 10 per cent for ease of calculations) change in one key factor at a time. We then trace the effect of the small change on net profit. We hold all other key factors constant except consequential changes such as movements in variable costs resulting from changes in the level of activity. Having ascertained the percentage change in the net profit we divide it by the change in the key factor to arrive at the profit multiplier. Thus if we increase the price level by 10 per cent, and this has the effect of raising the net profit by 60 per cent, our profit multiplier has a value of 6.0.

(c) Once we have calculated the PM values, we produce a ranking of the key factors based on the relative magnitudes of the profit multipliers. This will show the relative sensitivity of net profit to changes in the various key factors: the higher the PM value, the more sensitive the net profit to changes in the key factor concerned. It is from the ranking of the profit multipliers that we draw conclusions with regard to how the business makes its profits and the most fruitful areas for any possible profit improvement measures that might be contemplated by the business.

EXAMPLE 1

Students should note that the business in the first example operates at a fairly high level of fixed costs as administration and general expenses plus selling and distribution expenses amount to 60 per cent of the sales volume. Variable costs, on the other hand, are relatively low.

Set out below is a summary of the Profit and Loss Account of a manufacturing company in respect of Month 7.

Profit and Loss Account: Summary

No. of Units		10 000
Price per Unit		£10
Sales Revenue		£100 000
less Direct Materials	£10 000	
Direct Labour	15 000	
Direct Expenses	5 000	
Adm. & Gen. Expenses	40 000	
Sell. & Distr. Expenses	20 000	90 000
Net Profit		10 000

Solution

There are seven key factors in this case: on the revenue side we have: (a) the number of units and (b) the price level. On the cost side we have: (a) direct materials; (b) direct labour; (c) direct expenses; (d) administration and general expenses and (e) selling and distribution expenses.

Next we have to calculate a profit multiplier for each key factor as shown below.

No. of Units:	
Sales	£110 000
less Total Cost	93 000
Net Profit	17 000

We assumed a 10 per cent increase in the number of units, which gives us sales of £110 000. Total cost is now £93 000 which is the original £90 000 plus the consequential increase in variable costs of £3 000 (i.e. 10 per cent of direct materials, direct labour and direct expenses). The increase in net profit (from £10 000 to £17 000) is 70 per cent, following a 10 per cent increase in the number of units. Our profit multiplier is, therefore, 7.0.

Price Level:

Sales	£110 000
less Total Cost	90 000
Net Profit	£20 000

Only the price level has changed here and there is no other change. Total cost is therefore unchanged at £90 000. The net profit has increased (from £10 000 to £20 000) by 100 per cent, and this gives a profit multiplier of 10.0.

Direct Materials:

Sales	£100 000
less Total Cost	91 000
Net Profit	£ 9 000

In the above calculation there is no change on the revenue side. We have just assumed a change of 10 per cent in the cost of direct materials which has decreased net profit (from £10 000 to £9000) by 10 per cent. Our profit multiplier is, therefore, 1.0.

Direct Labour:

Sales	£100 000
less Total Cost	91 500
Net Profit	£ 8 500

Here again the only change is that in direct labour which reduces the net profit by 15 per cent and thus gives a profit multiplier of 1.5.

Direct Expenses:

Sales	£100 000
less Total Cost	90 500
Net Profit	£ 9 500

The assumed change in the direct expenses decreases the net profit by 5 per cent and results in a profit multiplier of 0.5.

Administration & General Expenses:

Sales	£100 000
less Total Cost	94 000
Net Profit	£ 6 000

The increase in the administration and general expenses of 10 per cent has the effect of decreasing the net profit by 40 per cent. The profit multiplier is, therefore, 4.0.

Selling and Distribution Expenses:

Sales	£100 000
less Total Cost	92 000
Net Profit	£ 8 500

Finally the increase in this last key factor of 10 per cent reduces the net profit by 20 per cent and results in a profit multiplier of 2.0.

A word of explanation is required before we proceed to the ranking of the profit multipliers. All the profit multipliers calculated for the cost-based key factors should, strictly speaking, be shown as negative values: -1.0, -1.5, etc. The minus signs in the context of profit sensitivity analysis are, however, of no consequence and are therefore ignored.

Ranking

Key factor	PM
Price Level	10.0
No. of Units	7.0
Adm. & Gen. Expenses	4.0
Sell. and Distr. Expenses	2.0
Direct labour	1.5
Direct Materials	1.0
Direct Expense	0.5

CONCLUSIONS

The first and most important conclusion from the PM profile is that the company has high profit multipliers on the revenue side of the business and relatively low profit multipliers on the cost side. This indicates that the revenue side of the business has a stronger impact on net profit than the cost side. We may, therefore, conclude that the company is market oriented rather than cost oriented.

The price level PM has a value of 10.0. This means that, other things being equal (i.e. assuming that there is no other change), every 1 per cent change in the price level will result in a 10 per cent change in net profit. Quite clearly, therefore, the pricing policy of the company has the most critical impact on its profitability. The number of units, i.e. the physical sales volume, is the next most important determinant of net profit. If, therefore, the company is not able to increase its price level then increasing the number of units sold will have a very similar effect: every 1 per cent increase in the number of units sold will, other things being equal, add 7 per cent to net profit.

On the cost side of the business both administration and general expenses and selling and distribution expenses have higher PM values than those for the three elements of the prime cost. Whilst the cost-based profit multipliers are relatively low in relation to those operating on the revenue side of the business, they still have an appreciable effect on the net profit and should therefore be subject to strict continual review.

From the point of view of accounting and control procedures the message of the PM profile here is loud and clear. The net profit of the company is very sensitive to changes on the revenue side of the business, and consequently cost control here is less effective in promoting profitability than the control of the sales revenue: regular and systematic reviews of the sales volume, sales mix, profit margins, pricing procedures, price adjustments, etc. need a great deal of the accountant's and manager's time and attention to ensure adequate profitability.

EXAMPLE 2

Students should note that in this second example we have a company operating at a high percentage (70 per cent) of variable costs.

Set out below is a summary of the Profit and Loss Account of a manufacturing company in respect of Month 7.

Profit and Loss Account: Summary

No. of Units		10 000
Price per Unit		£10
Sales Revenue		£100 000
less Direct Materials	£30 000	
Direct Labour	25 000	
Direct Expense	15 000	
Adm. and Gen. Expenses	10 000	
Sell. and Distr. Expenses	10 000	90 000
Net Profit		10 000

SOLUTION

As in the previous example we have altogether seven key factors – two on the revenue side and five on the cost side. The profit multipliers may be calculated as shown in the table below.

	Base Figures	Price	No. of Units	Direct Material	Direct Labour	Direct Expenses	Administration and General Expenses	Selling and Distribution Expenses
	£	£	£	£	£	£	£	£
Sales	100 000	110 000	110 000	100 000	100 000	100 000	100 000	100 000
Direct Materials	30 000	30 000	33 000	33 000	30 000	30 000	30 000	30 000
Direct Labour	25 000	25 000	27 500	25 000	27 500	25 000	25 000	25 000
Direct Expenses	15 000	15 000	16 500	15 000	15 000	16 500	15 000	15 000
Administration and General Expenses	10 000	10 000	10 000	10 000	10 000	10 000	11 000	10 000
Selling and Distribution Expenses	10 000	10 000	10 000	10 000	10 000	10 000	10 000	11 000
Total Cost	90 000	90 000	97 000	93 000	92 500	91 500	91 000	91 000
Net profit	10 000	20 000	13 000	7 000	7 500	8 500	9 000	9 000
% Change in NP	—	100.0	30.0	30.0	25.0	15.0	10.0	10.0
Profit Multiplier		10.0	3.0	3.0	2.5	1.5	1.0	1.0

From the table on page 135 our ranking of profit multipliers would be shown as follows.

Ranking

Key Factor	PM
Price Level	10.0
No. of Units	3.0
Direct Materials	3.0
Direct Labour	2.5
Direct Expenses	1.5
Administration and General Expenses	1.0
Selling and Distribution Expenses	1.0

CONCLUSIONS

The PM profile in this example is considerably different from that in Example 1. The main differences are as follows.

(a) Whilst in the first example there is a clear difference in the PM values between the cost side and the revenue side of the business, in Example 2 there is no evidence that the revenue side has a dominant effect on net profit.

(b) The prime cost has a combined PM value of (3.0 + 2.5 + 1.5) 7.0 and this is a clear indication that cost control is in this company of the utmost importance. Should, for some reason, the prime cost increase by 5 per cent, the net profit will, other things being equal, decrease by (5% × 7) 35 per cent.

(c) The company in Example 1 has a low level of variable costs and a high P/V ratio of 70 per cent. The company in Example 2 has high variable costs and a P/V ratio of 30 per cent. It is for this reason that the first No. of units PM is 7.0 whilst the second is only 3.0.

(d) The second company is clearly cost oriented and should pay a great deal of attention to cost control, whilst at the same time keeping an eye on its price level as this has the highest PM value.

■ MORE ABOUT PROFIT MULTIPLIERS

From what has been said so far students will appreciate that the profit multiplier is a catalyst which determines the quantitative effect on net profit of a change in a given key factor. We may represent diagrammatically the operation of the profit multiplier as in Fig. 15.

Fig. 15 *Operation of profit multiplier*

Let us revert to our Example 1 where a 5 per cent change in each of the key factors would have an impact on net profit as follows:

Key Factor	PM	% Change in Net Profit
Price Level	10.0	50.0
No. of Units	7.0	35.0
Administration and General Expenses	4.0	20.0
Selling and Distribution Expenses	2.0	10.0
Direct Labour	1.5	7.5
Direct Materials	1.0	5.0
Direct Expense	0.5	2.5

Our conclusion from the above example is that it is not so much the percentage change in the key factor as the relevant profit multiplier that determines the impact on net profit.

Whenever in our calculations we arrived at a profit multiplier we always used the assumption of 'other things being equal'. This does not mean that there may not be more than one change. It is simply an assumption which enables us to quantify the individual and full impact of one key factor. Thus if we assumed that: (a) there is a decrease in the price level and this immediately results in (b) a lower number of units sold, the resulting change in the net profit would have been caused by two key factors and the individual impact of either of them would not be known.

Profit multipliers and price level decisions

Profit multipliers may usefully be applied in price level decisions, particularly when it is necessary to devise a price revision strategy in a multi-product company. Let us assume that we have been given the following budgeted profit statement of a small trading company selling four products.

Budgeted Profit Statement

Product	Sales £	Variable Cost £	Contribution £
A	200 000	80 000	120 000
B	150 000	60 000	90 000
C	100 000	50 000	50 000
D	50 000	10 000	40 000
Total	500 000	200 000	300 000

less Fixed Administration, Selling and Distribution Expenses		220 000
Budgeted Net Profit		80 000

Let us now assume that the directors have decided that they are not satisfied with the budgeted net profit. They have asked the management accountant to suggest appropriate price level adjustments which will raise the budgeted net profit by at least 20% (i.e. to at least £96 000). It is assumed that an increase in the price level of any one product up to 5 per cent will not have an adverse effect on the number of units sold.

SOLUTION

Overall Price Level Profit Multiplier:

Sales	£550 000
less Total Cost	420 000
Net Profit	£130 000

Net profit has increased (from £80 000 to £130 000) by 62.5 per cent and the profit multiplier is 6.25.

Product A Price Level Profit Multiplier:

Sales	£520 000
less Total Cost	420 000
Net Profit	£100 000

The sales volume here consists of the original £500 000 plus the assumed 10 per cent change in the sales volume of Product A only. The increase in net profit is 25.0 per cent giving a profit multiplier of 2.50.

Product B Price Level Profit Multiplier:

Sales	£515 000
less Total Cost	420 000
Net Profit	£ 95 000

The increase in net profit amounts to 18.7 per cent giving a profit multiplier of 1.87.

Product C Price Level Profit Multiplier:

Sales	£510 000
less Total Cost	420 000
Net Profit	£ 90 000

Net profit has increased by 12.5 per cent and the profit multiplier is, therefore, 1.25.

Product D Price Level Profit Multiplier:

Sales	£505 000
less Total Cost	420 000
Net Profit	£ 85 000

The increase in net profit here amounts to 6.25 per cent, giving a profit multiplier of 0.63.

We may now check our calculations as follows:

Price Level PM – A	2.50
Price Level PM – B	1.87
Price Level PM – C	1.25
Price Level PM – D	0.63
Overall Price Level PM	6.25

Now that we have the price level profit multipliers for the four products, we may suggest several price level revision strategies as shown below.

Strategy A:

Increase Price of A by 4% × 2.50	=	10.0%
Increase Price of B by 3% × 1.87	=	5.6%
Increase Price of C by 4% × 1.25	=	5.0%
Leave Price of D unchanged		—
Increase in Budgeted Net Profit		20.6%

Strategy B:

Increase Price of A by 2% × 2.50	=	5.0%
Increase Price of B by 4% × 1.87	=	7.5%
Increase Price of C by 4% × 1.25	=	5.0%
Increase Price of D by 4% × 0.63	=	2.5%
Increase in Budgeted Net Profit		20.0%

Strategy C:

Increase Price of A by 3% × 2.50	=	7.5%
Increase Price of B by 5% × 1.87	=	9.4%
Increase Price of C by 2% × 1.25	=	2.5%
Increase Price of D by 1% × 0.63	=	0.6%
Increase in Budgeted Net Profit		20.0%

Students will realize that with this technique a very large number of price revision strategies may be devised. Also it should be noted that our price level adjustments are very small – yet they lead to a substantial overall increase in net profit.

■ SELF ASSESSMENT QUESTIONS

1 Explain what you understand by:
(a) profit multiplier;
(b) profit multiplier profile.
2 Discuss the relevance of the PM profile to cost control on the one hand and revenue control on the other.
3 How may one use the PM profile to determine whether a business is cost oriented or market oriented?
4 Set out below is the Profit and Loss Account Summary of a manufacturing company.

No. of Units		10 000
Price per Unit		£10
Sales Revenue		£100 000
less Direct Materials	£20 000	
Direct Labour	10 000	
Fixed Factory Overheads	20 000	
Administration and General Expenses	30 000	
Advertising and Sales Promotion Expenses	10 000	90 000
Net Profit		£ 10 000

You are required to calculate the profit multipliers, rank them in the order of magnitude and comment on the sensitivity of the net profit to the relevant key factors.

5 John Brown owns two small factories and given below are their summarized Profit and Loss Accounts for the year ended 31 December 19...

	A	B
No. of Units	10 000	20 000
Price per Unit	£20	£10
Sales Revenue	£200 000	£200 000
Variable Costs:		
Direct Materials	80 000	20 000
Direct Labour	50 000	30 000
Direct Expenses	20 000	10 000
Fixed Costs:		
Factory Overhead	15 000	40 000
Administration Expenses	10 000	30 000
Selling and Distribution Expenses	5 000	50 000
Total Cost	180 000	180 000
Net Profit	20 000	20 000

You are required to:
  (a) calculate the profit multipliers for two factories;
  (b) rank the profit multipliers;
  (c) comment on the differences between the two PM profiles with regard to possible improvements in profitability.

6   The ABC Trading Company sells three products and given below is a summary of the Budgeted Profit and Loss Account prepared by the management accountant.

Budgeted Profit and Loss Account Summary

Product	Sales	Variable Cost	Contribution
	£	£	£
A	500 000	200 000	300 000
B	300 000	150 000	150 000
C	200 000	100 000	100 000
Total	1 000 000	450 000	550 000

less Fixed Costs:		
Administration and General	200 000	
Selling Expenses	150 000	
Distribution Expenses	100 000	450 000
Budgeted Net Profit		100 000

You are informed that the directors of the company have decided that the budgeted profit of £100 000 is not adequate. They have asked you to suggest three different price level adjustment strategies which will increase the budgeted profit to £120 000. The directors insist, however, that the upward revision of individual product prices must be within 5 per cent.

7   The Trident Company Ltd is a trading organization with three branches: A, B and C. Set out below is a summary of the trading results for the year ended 31 December 19...

Profit and Loss Account – Summary

	Branch A	Branch B	Branch C	Total
	£000	£000	£000	£000
Sales	500	300	200	1 000
Variable Costs:				
Cost of Sales	280	170	110	560
Direct Labour	100	50	40	190
Fixed Costs:				
Management Salaries	40	30	20	90
Other Costs	30	20	10	60
	450	270	180	900
Branch Operating Profit	50	30	20	100
less Head Office Expenses				50
Net Profit				50

In view of the poor results achieved during the last year of trading management have called a meeting to discuss ways and means of improving the net profit for the following year. The following comments have been made.

(a) Managing Director: 'We face extremely keen competititon and it is imperative that any price increase is kept within 5 per cent.'

(b) Branch A Manager: 'My cost controls are very strict and there is no prospect of improving the profitability of my branch through cost savings. The only thing I can do is raise my prices by 5 per cent.'

(c) Branch B Manager: 'In my area competition is extremely keen. What I will do, however, is to try and save 5 per cent on my cost of sales.'

(d) Branch C Manager: 'We operate a strict system of stores control and a price increase is just not on. I can only save 5 per cent of my direct labour and management salaries.'

The managing director insists that the net profit should be doubled next year. You are required to calculate appropriate profit multipliers and:

(a) state what overall net profit would be achieved if the branch managers were to go ahead with their suggestions as in (b), (c) and (d) above.

(b) state what net profit would be achieved if the only change next year was an overall price increase of 5 per cent.

(c) state, giving reasons, which course of action is preferable.

8   The Leisure Complex Company Ltd operates a leisure complex which consists of three profit centres: a gymnasium and swimming pool, a restaurant and a gift shop. Set out below is a summarized Profit and Loss Account of the company for the year ended 31 December 19... .

Profit and Loss Account

	Net Sales	Cost of Sales	Wages and Salaries	Dept Profit
	£000	£000	£000	£000
Gymnasium and Swimming Pool	600	50	150	400
Restaurant	400	140	160	100
Gift Shop	200	110	20	70
	1 200	300	330	570
less Administration and General Expenses				490
Net Profit				80

You are required, in your capacity as management accountant to:

(a) calculate the profit multipliers for the three profit centres;

(b) make preliminary suggestions as to which elements (sales, cost of sales, direct labour, etc.) offer potential for profit improvement. State clearly any assumptions you have to make.

13 | Pricing

■ IMPORTANCE OF PRICING

The study of pricing is, primarily, of interest to students of marketing. Nevertheless students of accounting – and management accounting in particular – should have a good knowledge of pricing for several reasons.

Management accountants, even though they may not actually make the pricing decision, are closely involved in the pricing process:

1 They advise on basic costing procedures, including the allocation and apportionment of costs and, in this way, exercise discretion in the area of unit costs of various products. The cost per unit is in many industries taken as a base from which to calculate the selling price.

2 Management accountants advise on product profit margins and their judgement will necessarily have quite considerable influence on the structure and overall level of prices charged.

3 In many organizations (particularly those manufacturing a wide range of products and using the absorption pricing method) the pricing decision is virtually the province of the management accountant, who decides on product prices almost as a matter of routine.

It is for these reasons that the student of management accounting should regard pricing as one of the most important areas of study. The subject matter of Chapter 12 is also relevant in this context. It will be recalled that of all the profit multipliers, the price level profit multiplier is always the one with the highest value. In other words, of all the key factors normally associated with business operations (price, direct materials, direct labour, direct expenses, etc.) the price level profit multiplier is always the most powerful in terms of the impact on net profit. And this is the most obvious reason why all students of business administration – and particularly those studying marketing and/or management accounting – should have a good knowledge of pricing.

Finally pricing is important because of the generally wide impact of the price level. The price level influences much more than just profitability. It affects the number of units sold, i.e. the physical volume of sales; it influences profits available for dividends; it affects the cash available for new plant, machinery, etc.

■ ROLE OF COSTS IN PRICING

Accountants, and especially cost accountants, have traditionally over-emphasized the role of costs in pricing. To the accountant cost is something real, almost tangible – something which is easily ascertainable by reference to purchase invoices, cost sheets, etc. Cost, therefore, has tended to be the most important criterion in the pricing of (particularly) manufactured products. Yet, on reflection, it is clear that the role of costs in pricing is neither as important nor as obvious as might be assumed.

In industries which operate at a high percentage of fixed/indirect costs, the definition of 'cost' presents a problem. Thus it may cost £10 000 a week to operate a theatre. During some parts of the year the number of patrons may average 2 000 a week – when the 'cost per unit' will be £5.00. During slack periods the number of patrons may be as low as 1 000 per week – with a 'cost per unit' of £10.00. Indeed, the number of patrons may vary significantly from one day to another. What, in such circumstances, is the true 'cost per unit'?

Students should appreciate that the importance of cost in the context of pricing depends primarily on the composition of total cost, i.e. the respective proportions of fixed/indirect costs on the one hand, and variable/direct costs on the other. Thus in retailing operations the direct cost is generally high. If we sell a pound of coffee, costing £4.00, for £5.00, the direct cost is a strong, substantial and meaningful base for fixing the price and the relationship between price and cost is direct and obvious. If, on the other hand we sell a hotel room costing (in terms of direct supplies such as linen, soap, etc.) £3.00 for £60.00, the link between cost and price is weak, vague and indirect. Indeed, it is doubtful that, in this kind of situation, direct cost has any bearing on the price charged.

In the area of professional services the relationship between cost and price is tenuous. A medical practitioner may well charge very different fees for performing the same kind of operation on two different patients. When a famous conductor asks for a fee of £1 000 per concert, it is difficult to imagine how this may have been arrived at in terms of cost considerations. One would suspect that the fee is based on the conductor's reputation and has nothing to do with the cost (time taken, etc.) of providing this service.

The relationship between cost and price is also blurred by the demand for the product/service as well as the nature of the product/service. In the case of perishable products price will respond to demand patterns rather than changes on the cost side. A shopkeeper who finds, late on Saturday afternoon, that there still remains unsold 50lbs of strawberries will, in all probability, wish to sell the remaining stock even at half price to avoid complete loss through deterioration. A single journey by rail from A to B will depend on the time of day and on whether the traveller has some kind of season ticket or is an occasional traveller.

From all the examples given above it should be clear that cost is not the only nor, indeed, the most important determinant of price. Pricing decisions, though sometimes based on cost, are complex and influenced by a large variety of factors as discussed below.

■ DETERMINANTS OF PRICING

Our approach to pricing, i.e. our pricing philosophy, pricing strategy as well as pricing tactics, will depend on a large number of factors some of which are discussed below.

Cost structure

In industries operating at a high percentage of fixed/indirect costs, the variable/direct costs will by definition be low; and in such circumstances the price will tend to reflect the market situation (competition, type of customer, trends in sales, etc.) rather than operating costs. In high variable/direct cost industries (e.g. in retailing operations where the direct cost is very high) the price will tend to reflect the cost of the product – though naturally it will have been fixed after taking into account the reality of the market place.

Demand

The demand for a product/service may be described in terms of its elasticity. Demand is said to be elastic where the quantity purchased is responsive to the price. Conversely, where the quantity purchased is little influenced by price, demand is said to be inelastic. This is illustrated in Fig. 16(a) and (b).

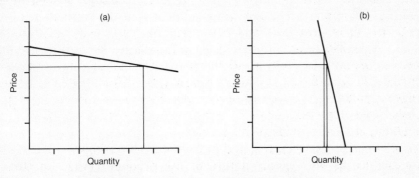

Fig. 16 *Elastic and inelastic demand*

Elasticity of demand is determined by a number of factors, but the most important of these is the availability of substitutes. Where substitutes are good demand is elastic, and vice versa. Elasticity of demand is mainly relevant to short-term price manipulations and adjustments (i.e. pricing tactics). Bread has no effective substitute and, in consequence, the local baker would stand little to gain by lowering the price of bread. What the baker would lose in terms of price would not be compensated by the extra number of loaves sold – see Fig. 16(b).

There are numerous types of motor vehicle available and many of them are similar in a number of respects and are, therefore, effective substitutes. If one manufacturer were to lower the price it is quite likely that this would result in a significant number of additional cars sold – see Fig. 16(a).

Customer profile

In order to evolve the right price policy we must consider the customer profile. Indeed many marketing experts would say that this is one of the most important determinants of price policy. The customers of a business may belong to different socio-economic groups, they may be manual workers, professional persons, poor, rich, young, old, etc. And, quite clearly, the type of customer we wish to attract must necessarily influence our approach to pricing as, indeed, the nature of the product itself.

Nature of product

The nature of the product will also have considerable influence on the approach to pricing. A company which is introducing a new product, which is a novelty, will often assume that the demand for the product will be short-lived. The price of the product will then be set at a high level on the assumption that it is important to 'make hay whilst the sun shines'. The approach to the pricing of well-established products is frequently quite different in that the aims of the seller may be to ensure widespread acceptance of the product through a reasonably low price.

Some products are homogeneous (identical), others are heterogenous (differentiated). When a homogeneous product is being sold by a number of sellers, price differences from one seller to another will tend to be minimal. A bottle of a particular brand of gin will sell at practically the same price from one shop to another. Where a product is differentiated, however, most sellers will be able to pursue an independent price policy and charge significantly different prices. The dental treatment offered by Dentist A may appear to be different from that offered by Dentist B – with the result that both will tend to charge considerably different fees. Lunch at a Chinese restaurant is a different kind of experience from lunch at an Italian restaurant – both establishments will be free to charge very different prices and indeed strive to stress the differences between the two products.

Finally products vary in terms of their perishability and durability. The storage of durable products presents no major problems – indeed if we do not sell a suite of furniture today we may well sell it next month at a higher price. With perishable products, including services (e.g. theatre seats, hotel rooms, public areas in museums, etc.) the price charged has to reflect demand patterns; and reflect not only long-term annual trends but also daily and weekly patterns of business.

Profits required

Most certainly one of the most important considerations in pricing is the achievement of satisfactory profits. When deciding on the general price level of an enterprise, a great deal of thought must be given to the desired net profit. As mentioned earlier in this chapter, the price level has a most pervasive influence on profitability and its importance cannot be over-emphasized.

Spare capacity

A large proportion of businesses experience seasonal or otherwise wholly unpredictable fluctuations in demand – with the result that over varying periods of time they experience significant spare capacity. The existence of spare capacity – a phenomenon more common than is probably generally recognized – has a great deal of relevance to pricing tactics. As explained in Chapter 4, pricing during slack periods is different in that it is possible and profitable to price products below 'total cost'. All seasonal businesses and those subject to pronounced weekly patterns of business tend to adopt a complex pricing policy which reflects changes in the intensity of demand. This is particularly true in situations where the business operates at a high level of fixed costs.

We have mentioned a fair number of examples of factors which influence the firm's approach to pricing. We could have mentioned many more, as the number of such influencing factors is very large indeed.

■ THE PRICING SITUATION

In spite of the great multiplicity of factors influencing pricing policy, it is possible to categorize them and place them all under three major headings. Whatever the cost structure, demand, nature of product, type of customer, etc. all the influencing factors may be placed under the following headings: (a) operating costs, (b) market situation and (c) business objectives. This is illustrated in Fig. 17.

Given the objectives of the business the pricing situation will be largely dependent on either the cost side or the revenue side. Thus businesses operating at a high proportion of variable costs (e.g. retailers) will find themselves in a cost oriented pricing situation and will tend to use cost based pricing methods. Those which have a high proportion of fixed costs (e.g. theatres) will be in a revenue/market oriented pricing situation and will tend to use revenue/market oriented pricing methods. Of course there will always be grey areas – situations which are neither fully cost nor fully market oriented. Finally there are

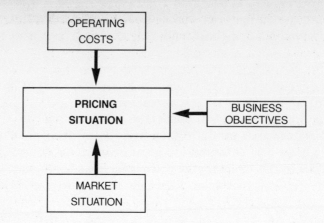

Fig. 17 *The pricing situation*

organizations which view pricing as, essentially, an instrument for securing the right profitability. These will tend to use the rate of return pricing method – a method which is profit oriented.

Students should appreciate that when we refer to one pricing orientation or another, we are not speaking of distinctly and wholly different things. A business which is in a cost oriented situation will naturally pay enough attention to the forces of the market. Equally, one which is in a market oriented pricing situation will, when formulating its price policy, pay attention to operating costs. Pricing orientations relate to the general approach and the balance of emphasis; and a given orientation does not exclude a consideration of other factors which may be relevant.

■ CONVENTIONAL PRICING METHODS

Cost-plus pricing

The cost-plus method of pricing is used extensively in a number of industries; it is particularly popular in retailing. The method works as follows:

1 We calculate the direct cost per unit – this is, typically, the unit purchase price shown on the supplier's invoice.

2 We then add what is described as a 'fair rate of gross profit' to arrive at the selling price. The fair rate of gross profit is normally a percentage of gross profit which will vary from one trade/industry to another. The percentage of profit added must be adequate to cover the operating expenses and also leave a satisfactory margin of net profit.

Within a particular business operation a number of different rates (percentages) of gross profit may be used. A dealer in furniture, for example, may price bedroom furniture on the basis of cost plus 30 per cent; reproduction antique furniture at cost plus 50 per cent and carpets at cost plus 40 per cent. As a general rule, luxury goods and slow-moving items tend to attract a higher rate of gross profit than fast-moving necessities such as food products.

The main advantage of the cost-plus method is that it is simple and easy to apply. Also there are no complications (such as encountered in absorption pricing) with the apportionment of indirect costs. The method has, however, several disadvantages. First, in its crude form, the cost-plus method is cost oriented and therefore ignores the demand for the product/service. Secondly with this method of pricing net profit is dependent on the volume of sales, and is not related to the capital of the business. In other words, the more we sell the higher the net profit, but there is no guarantee that, at the end of the year, net profit will be correct as a percentage of capital employed. Finally, where there are several products, the right percentage of gross profit may be difficult to fix. Some products may be expensive in terms of labour. Others may be expensive to store if, for instance, they require costly storage and/or refrigeration facilities. Whatever the objections to cost-plus pricing, the method is very popular and if used intelligently (i.e. with due regard to the market place and aspects of profitability) can prove an easy and satisfactory method of pricing.

Rate of return pricing

The rate of return pricing method is neither cost nor market oriented – its aim is to secure the right relationship between net profit and capital employed; it is, therefore, profit oriented. The method works as follows:

1   We calculate the capital employed and fix the profit target. The profit target is usually expressed as a percentage, and therefore where the capital employed is £1 000 000 we may decide that net profit should be £150 000, i.e. 15 per cent.
2   Secondly we predict/predetermine the sales volume and calculate the net profit margin. To continue the previous example, we may decide that our sales volume will be £1 500 000, so to reach our profit target of £150 000, our net profit margin should be 10 per cent.
3   Having completed 1 and 2 above, we then arrange our costs, profit margins and selling prices in such a manner as to ensure the achievement of the profit target.

The main advantage of rate of return pricing is its orientation. The main objective of the business enterprise is the achievement of a satisfactory return on capital, which is facilitated by this particular pricing method. Secondly, as will be seen later in this chapter, we may use rate of return pricing in conjunction with other pricing methods, e.g. cost-plus, absorption pricing, etc.

EXAMPLE

A national retailing organization is planning a new department store for a provincial city. From preliminary investigations it is estimated that the capital required for the new venture will amount to £5 000 000. Also it is estimated that the turnover of the new store will amount to £10 000 000. The directors of the company require a return on capital of 20 per cent before tax. Preliminary overall figures have been produced as below.

	£000
Sales	10 000
less Costs of Goods Sold	7 000
Gross Profit	3 000
less Direct Labour	1 400
Management Salaries	200
Operating Expenses	300
Fixed Charges	100
	2 000
Net Profit	1 000

After detailed consideration of the probable sales mix and the customary profit margins, the following pattern of sales, sales mix and profit margins has been prepared.

Department	Sales		Cost of sales		Gross profit	
	£000	%	£000	%	£000	%
Food	4 050	40.5	3 000	74.1	1 050	25.9
Furniture	3 000	30.0	2 000	66.7	1 000	33.3
Cosmetics	850	8.5	500	58.8	350	41.2
Carpets	2 100	21.0	1 500	71.4	600	28.6
Total	10 000	100.0	7 000	70.0	3 000	30.0

From the above table it may be seen that in order to achieve the profit target of 20 per cent, the store will have to secure gross profit margins (in relation to sales) of:

Food   –   25.9% of sales
Furniture –   33.3% of sales
Cosmetics –   41.2% of sales
Carpets   –   28.6% of sales

In practical day-to-day cost-plus pricing the required percentage of gross profit is normally added to the unit cost, which is taken as the base, i.e. 100 per cent. From this point of view our pricing procedure would be:
1   Food – gross profit of £1 050 000 is equal to 35 per cent of the cost of sales of £3 000 000. A product which costs £1.00 would therefore be priced at £1.35.

The gross profit margin of 35 per cent is thus equal to the 25.9 per cent gross profit on selling price.

2 Furniture – the gross profit of £1 000 000 is equal to 50 per cent of the cost of sales of £2 000 000. An item of furniture purchased for £100 would therefore be priced at £150.

3 Cosmetics – the gross profit here is £350 000 and this is equal to 70 per cent of the cost of sales. Thus a bottle of perfume purchased at £10 would be expected to sell for £17.

4 Carpets – in this particular case, the gross profit of £600 000 represents 40 per cent of the cost of sales of £1 500 000. A carpet purchased at £100 would be expected to fetch £140.

Students should appreciate that in the above example we have combined the rate of return method with the cost-plus method. Our basic aim was to secure the achievement of the profit target of £1 000 000; and if: (a) we price all the products according to the formula evolved; (b) secure the desired sales volume and sales mix and (c) control the cost of labour and other expenses, we can be sure of achieving the desired aim.

Contribution pricing

Contribution pricing is a relatively new pricing method, which has gained popularity in recent years. The method works as follows:

1 The first and most important step is to divide all costs as between those which are fully fixed and those which are fully variable.

2 The second step is to ascertain for each unit of output the variable cost per unit.

3 We then add an appropriate amount of contribution to the variable cost per unit to arrive at the selling price.

4 No attempt is made to apportion fixed/indirect costs to individual units of output.

Contribution pricing offers a number of advantages – especially in the area of short-term or tactical pricing. When business is slack it is sometimes necessary/advantageous to quote prices below 'total cost'. With contribution pricing, the variable cost per unit indicates the lowest acceptable short-run price. Any price over and above the variable cost per unit is going to produce some contribution and is, therefore, worth while. Students should remember that with other methods of pricing, e.g. absorption pricing, no distinction is made between the fixed and variable components of the cost of a product. Whenever, therefore, it is necessary to quote a special, low price, the lowest acceptable price is not immediately apparent. Contribution pricing is particularly suitable in situations where there is a lot of turbulence in the market place resulting in price instability. In such circumstances it is essential for the business to be able to respond to such instability in terms of appropriate pricing tactics. It should, however, be remembered that contribution pricing has one major disadvantage.

In situations where sales representatives are allowed to offer low prices, discounts and special price concessions, there is the danger that they may secure an impressive volume of sales, some contribution but not enough of it for the business to cover its fixed costs. Any price reductions, special prices, etc. should, therefore, be subject to strict scrutiny: otherwise the benefits of contribution pricing may well be severely prejudiced. All sales staff and others concerned should, therefore, be acutely aware of the distinction between the basic, normal price at which the products should be sold as a matter of ordinary daily routine and special reduced prices which should only be offered in special circumstances.

Absorption pricing

Absorption pricing is one of the oldest pricing methods in use and is particularly popular in manufacturing companies where it has been practised for many decades. It is known as absorption pricing because each unit of output 'absorbs', in addition to its direct cost, some indirect costs, e.g. factory overheads. Absorption pricing flows directly from the process of absorption costing described in Chapter 5.

It will be remembered that the most important stages of the absorption process are:

1   The allocation and apportionment of costs to all production cost and service cost centres.
2   The transfer of service cost centre costs to production cost centres.
3   The allotment of costs from production cost centres to the individual units of output.

After the completion of the above process the next step is to add to each unit of output, a rate of profit which will then give the selling price. The rate/percentage of profit so added must be adequate to cover the indirect cost centres (e.g. administration, marketing costs) and leave a sufficient margin of net profit.

Students should realize that prices fixed in accordance with this method have two important characteristics. First, such prices are very cost oriented in that the price of each unit of output flows from the mechanics of cost allocation and cost apportionment; no account is taken of the realities of the market place. Secondly, such prices are rigid and inflexible as no attempt is made in this pricing method to distinguish between the fixed and variable elements of the cost of each unit of output. With absorption pricing, therefore, the quotation of special reduced prices, quantity discounts, etc. is difficult: the cost per unit does not provide any guide as to the lowest acceptable price.

Absorption pricing, although widely practised in many manufacturing industries, does not provide the cost information required for imaginative pricing tactics. However, proponents of the method maintain that its advantage is that it ensures the recovery of indirect costs.

Backward pricing

Backward pricing is not a method of pricing, but, rather, a method of adjusting operating costs to a fixed price. In several industries the price of a product/service is announced/published in advance, and the seller is obliged to accept all the business at that price. Thus many estate agents advertise their services at a fixed percentage fee. Some restaurants operate fixed price menus and advertise meals at an inclusive price of £x.

In such circumstances the need for a pricing mechanism does not exist from one day/week to another – the price has already been fixed. What the seller has to do is: (a) predict the sales volume at that price; (b) arrange the operating costs and profit margins in such a way as to ensure the right level of net profit.

Range of price discretion

The concept of the range of price discretion is relevant to our consideration of short-term tactical pricing earlier in this chapter. The range of price discretion is a short-run concept, relevant to that period of time during which fixed costs remain fixed, and is illustrated in Fig. 18.

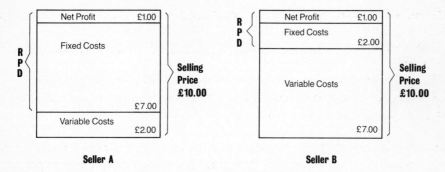

Fig. 18   *Range of price discretion*

Let us assume that there are two sellers, A and B. Both sell a product at £10.00 per unit, but the cost structure of each business is different. In the case of Seller A fixed costs amount to £7.00 per unit and variable costs £2.00 per unit. In the case of Seller B fixed costs amount to £2.00 and variable costs £7.00 per unit. In the short run the fixed costs of A and B will remain fixed; and any price in excess of variable cost will produce some contribution. Thus, in the short run, Seller A may charge any price between £2.00 and £10.00. This range of price discretion is very wide in that there is a multiplicity of prices that may profitably be charged. Seller B must, even in the short run, charge at least £7.00 per unit; and therefore his range of price discretion is relatively narrow.

It will be appreciated that the wider the range of price discretion the wider the range of prices that may be charged in the short run and, consequently, the more complex the pricing problem and, indeed, the greater the scope for imaginative pricing. Industries which operate at a high percentage of fixed costs – and consequently have a wide range of price discretion – tend to have a more complex structure of prices than those which operate at a high percentage of variable costs.

■ SELF ASSESSMENT QUESTIONS

1 Assess the role of costs in pricing – both generally and by reference to any three industries with which you are familiar.
2 Explain what you understand by cost orientation and market orientation.
3 Write an essay on the importance of pricing from the point of view of profit sensitivity analysis.
4 Explain the difference between cost oriented and market oriented pricing.
5 Your company is to import a new product, costing £10, and market it in the South East where the necessary premises and equipment have been acquired for £200 000.

The product will be marketed by sales representatives who will work on a commission-only basis of 25% of sales price, set at £20. Annual running costs of the new operation are estimated at £25 000.

Required:
   (a) A calculation of the number of units of the product that must be sold by the new division to earn the 30% required rate of return on the Head Office initial outlay.
   (b) An advertising agency has reviewed your product and states that for an expenditure of £15 000 on advertising a sales increase of 20 000 units could be confidently anticipated. Calculate whether the extra expenditure is justified.
   (c) A calculation of the effect of reducing the unit selling price by £1 on profits and the level of additional unit sales required to make this price reduction worth while.
                                            (Association of Business Executives)
6 Explain the concept of the range of price discretion.
7 Write explanatory notes on the following methods of pricing:
   (a) cost-plus pricing;
   (b) rate of return pricing;
   (c) contribution pricing;
   (d) absorption pricing;
   (e) backward pricing.
8 'The firm should continue in production as long as price is in excess of marginal cost.' What is the time scale implicit in this quotation?
9 Explain what you understand by 'pricing below total cost'. In what circumstances is it justified?
10 'A sound pricing strategy is one which is cost, market and profit oriented.' Explain.

14 | Responsibility accounting

■ INTRODUCTION

In Chapter 6 we made several references to ideas and concepts relevant to the present chapter. We explained that budgetary control assigns responsibility to executives; we illustrated some typical budgets and stressed the important relationship between authority and responsibility for operating results. The aim of the present chapter is to develop the idea of executive responsibility further and to introduce the student to the concept of responsibility accounting.

Effective control of business operations necessitates the development of a sound and streamlined organizational framework, within which each executive's role is defined in a clear and unambiguous manner. This can only be achieved by establishing what are known as *responsibility centres* and defining, in relation to each centre, the responsibility of each executive concerned.

A responsibility centre is a segment of the organization which may consist of a large department, employing dozens or hundreds of individuals (e.g. maintenance department of a large factory, sales department of a national distribution organization), or a small section/department employing a few individuals (foreign currency department in a bank, public relations department of a provincial city). In practice responsibility centres are relatively easy to develop. Thus in a big department store we may regard all the sales outlets (furniture department, food department, DIY department, etc.) as responsibility centres, each in the charge of a departmental manager responsible for the operating results. Other departments such as accounts, marketing, personnel and training, etc, would also constitute separate responsibility centres for which responsibility would have to be accepted by the chief accountant, marketing director and personnel and training manager respectively. Responsibility centres may be of three different types which are discussed below.

Cost centres

A cost centre is a responsibility centre where costs are incurred but where the manager has no control over revenue. In practice departments such as the accounts department, personnel and training department, maintenance department, etc. would be regarded as cost centres: they incur costs but, however important their contribution to the success of the business operation, they have no control over its sales revenue.

Profit centres

A profit centre is a responsibility centre where the manager has responsibility for controlling costs and revenue. Profit centres are of two types. In some, the majority of profit centres, the revenue is earned outside the business, i.e. in the market place. This type of profit centre is described as a *natural profit centre*. In other cases a profit centre may earn its revenue by 'selling' its output within the organization, e.g. to another department. This kind of profit centre is described as an *artificial profit centre*; and the price at which it sells its product/output within the organization is known as a *transfer price*.

Let us look at two examples of artificial profit centres from two very different types of business operation. In chemical engineering it is often found that the manufacture of a given product entails several distinctly different processes. The output of Process A is transferred to Process B from where it is transferred to Process C, etc. In order to ascertain the profit made by each process it is necessary to fix a transfer price at each transfer point; and it is at this price that each process 'sells' its output to the next process.

A restaurant company operating a chain of steak houses may decide that, instead of allowing the individual units to purchase their own meat, it would be cheaper to set up a central butchering department, buy the meat in bulk and then 'sell' it in smaller quantities – say at cost, plus 15 per cent – to the individual steak houses.

Students should note that, with artificial profit centres, the profits shown by the profit centres are somewhat unreal in that the revenue of the profit centre is the result of an assumed formula (agreed transfer price) rather than exposure to the realities of the market place. To revert to our two examples, the profit shown by Process B will depend on the transfer price at which it buys its input from Process A, and the transfer price for its own output sold to Process C. Similarly the profit achieved by the central butchering department will to a large extent depend on the transfer price at which the meat is sold to the individual steak houses. Whatever the profits shown by the various artificial profit centres the total profit of the company as a whole will still be the same. It should, however, be pointed out that artificial profit centres are effective in promoting motivation in that each manager can see the importance of the profit centre for which he has responsibility and its contribution – however calculated – to overall profits.

Investment centres

An investment centre is a type of responsibility centre in which the manager has the role of a chief executive and is responsible not only for his or her costs and revenue but also for the return on capital employed. An investment centre is, therefore, treated as if it were a separate autonomous business enterprise. The criterion most commonly employed in assessing the performance of an investment centre is the return on capital employed – already explained in Chapter 8.

EXAMPLE

We have now described the three types of responsibility centre; and it will be useful, at this stage, to relate these concepts to a practical situation. Let us assume that a medium-sized company operates three departmental stores, A, B and C, and that the organization chart of the company is as shown in Fig. 19.
We may divide the total operation into responsibility centres as follows.

The managing director is the chief executive of the company. He or she interprets the major aspects of policy as laid down by the board of directors and provides the link between the board and all the divisions/departments of the business. As chief executive, the managing director would be expected to accept responsibility for all costs, revenue and, indeed, the return on capital employed. The managing director would, therefore, accept responsibility for the total operation of the company as an investment centre.

The operations director would normally have responsibility for all costs and revenue and his/her performance would be assessed by reference to the net profit margin of the three stores. There might, however, be circumstances in which he or she would be expected to accept responsibility for the three stores as an investment centre. As a general principle, the more de-centralized the total company operation and the more authority given to an operations director, the greater the likelihood that he or she would be expected to assume responsibility for return on capital.

The general managers of the three stores would, typically, have responsibility for their operating costs and revenues, and each store would be regarded as a profit centre.

The departmental managers would not be regarded as responsible for profit centres, except in very large stores where each department employs a large number of persons and has a substantial volume of sales. Where that is so, it would be important to ensure that each departmental manager's responsibility is clearly defined and limited to the elements which are, in fact, controllable. Thus the departmental managers would be expected to accept responsibility for the volume of departmental sales, but – as they have no control over rates of pay – not for departmental payroll.

The purchasing director would have no control over the revenue of the stores; and the purchasing department would, clearly, be regarded as a cost centre.

The marketing director would share responsibility for the total sales volume of the stores with the general managers. Otherwise, for all practical purposes, the marketing department would be regarded as a cost centre.

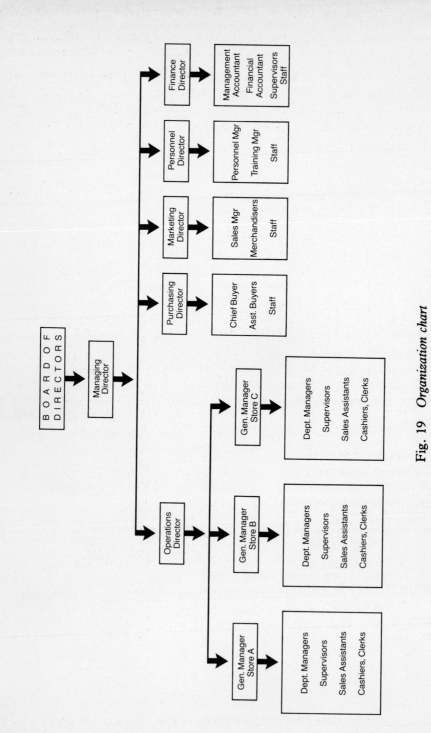

Fig. 19 *Organization chart*

The personnel director would, quite clearly, be seen as responsible for a cost centre.

The finance director although, no doubt, making a significant contribution to the profitability of the company, would also be regarded as responsible for a cost centre.

Let us now look at some of the more practical accounting aspects of responsibility accounting. All budgets, reports and accounting documents should reflect the principles of responsibility accounting and be drawn up in a manner which recognizes the existence of the relevant responsibility centres.

EXAMPLE

An example of a company operating three stores follows, showing a suggested format of a profit and loss account.

The ABC Retail Co.
Profit and Loss Account for year ended ....

Profit Centre	Net Sales	Cost of Sales	Wages and Salaries	Operating Expenses	Store Profit
	£000	£000	£000	£000	£000
Store A	5 000	3 000	500	450	1 050
Store B	3 000	1 750	325	275	650
Store C	2 000	1 150	175	125	550
	10 000	5 900	1 000	850	2 250

less Cost Centre Expenses:

Purchasing Department	180	20	
Marketing Department	150	210	
Personnel Department	110	40	
Finance Department	160	30	
	600	300	900

Profit before Fixed Charges — 1 350

less Company Fixed Charges:

Accountancy Fees	50	
Insurances	80	
Interest	170	
Sundry Fixed Charges	50	350

Net Profit before Tax — £1 000

The Profit and Loss Account consists of three parts. The top portion shows the operating results of the three stores, which are treated as natural profit centres.

From the net sales of each store we deduct the relevant figure of cost of sales, store wages and salaries as well as those operating expenses which are capable of being controlled by the store general manager. The resulting figure of store profit is, so to speak, the controllable profit of the store.

The middle portion of the Profit and Loss Account shows the expenses of the four cost centres. In respect of each of these we show the departmental wages and salaries and those operating expenses which are capable of being controlled within the cost centre.

Finally, in the third, lower, part of the Profit and Loss Account we deduct various company fixed charges which are incurred on behalf of the business as a whole and not for the benefit of any one cost or profit centre.

Students will note that, with this layout of the Profit and Loss Account, the aspect of executive responsibility for profit performance and cost control is given a great deal of prominence.

■ SELF ASSESSMENT QUESTIONS

1 Explain what you understand by responsibility accounting.

2 Write short, explanatory notes on:

(a) cost centre;

(b) profit centre;

(c) investment centre.

3 Distinguish clearly between natural profit centres and artificial profit centres. Give two examples of each.

4 Define responsibility accounting and describe the main features of a responsibility accounting system.

(Association of Business Executives – Modified)

5 Draw an organization chart of any type of business with which you are familiar, and:

(a) suggest how it might be divided into responsibility centres;

(b) draft a pro forma Profit and Loss Account, showing clearly the areas of executive responsibility for operating results.

Appendix

Table A Present value of £1.00 received in the future

Periods Hence	1%	2%	4%	6%	8%	10%	12%	14%	15%	16%	18%	20%	22%	24%	25%	26%	28%	30%	35%	40%
1	0.990	0.980	0.962	0.943	0.926	0.909	0.893	0.877	0.870	0.862	0.847	0.833	0.820	0.806	0.800	0.794	0.781	0.769	0.741	0.714
2	0.980	0.961	0.925	0.890	0.857	0.826	0.797	0.769	0.756	0.743	0.718	0.694	0.672	0.650	0.640	0.630	0.610	0.592	0.549	0.510
3	0.971	0.942	0.889	0.840	0.794	0.751	0.712	0.675	0.658	0.641	0.609	0.579	0.551	0.524	0.512	0.500	0.477	0.455	0.406	0.364
4	0.961	0.924	0.855	0.792	0.735	0.683	0.636	0.592	0.572	0.552	0.516	0.482	0.451	0.423	0.410	0.397	0.373	0.350	0.301	0.260
5	0.951	0.906	0.822	0.747	0.681	0.621	0.567	0.519	0.497	0.476	0.437	0.402	0.370	0.341	0.328	0.315	0.291	0.269	0.223	0.186
6	0.942	0.883	0.790	0.705	0.630	0.564	0.507	0.456	0.432	0.410	0.370	0.335	0.303	0.275	0.262	0.250	0.227	0.207	0.165	0.133
7	0.933	0.871	0.760	0.665	0.583	0.513	0.452	0.400	0.376	0.354	0.314	0.279	0.249	0.222	0.210	0.198	0.178	0.159	0.122	0.095
8	0.923	0.853	0.731	0.627	0.540	0.467	0.404	0.351	0.327	0.305	0.266	0.233	0.204	0.179	0.168	0.157	0.139	0.123	0.091	0.068
9	0.914	0.837	0.703	0.592	0.500	0.424	0.361	0.308	0.284	0.263	0.225	0.194	0.167	0.144	0.134	0.125	0.108	0.094	0.067	0.048
10	0.905	0.820	0.676	0.558	0.463	0.386	0.322	0.270	0.247	0.227	0.191	0.162	0.137	0.116	0.107	0.099	0.085	0.073	0.050	0.035
11	0.890	0.801	0.650	0.527	0.429	0.350	0.287	0.237	0.215	0.195	0.162	0.135	0.112	0.094	0.086	0.079	0.066	0.056	0.037	0.025
12	0.857	0.788	0.625	0.497	0.397	0.319	0.257	0.208	0.187	0.168	0.137	0.112	0.092	0.076	0.069	0.062	0.052	0.043	0.027	0.018
13	0.879	0.778	0.601	0.469	0.368	0.290	0.229	0.182	0.163	0.145	0.116	0.093	0.075	0.061	0.055	0.050	0.040	0.033	0.020	0.013
14	0.870	0.758	0.577	0.442	0.340	0.263	0.205	0.160	0.141	0.125	0.099	0.078	0.062	0.049	0.044	0.039	0.032	0.025	0.015	0.009
15	0.861	0.748	0.555	0.417	0.315	0.239	0.183	0.140	0.123	0.108	0.084	0.067	0.051	0.040	0.035	0.031	0.025	0.020	0.011	0.006

Index